THE SHAKESPEARE PARALLEL TEXT SERIES, THIRD EDITION

# Macbeth

by William Shakespeare

**Perfection Learning© Corporation**
**Logan, Iowa 51546-0500**

| | |
|---|---|
| **Editorial Director** | Julie A. Schumacher |
| **Senior Editor** | Rebecca Christian |
| **Series Editor** | Rebecca Burke |
| **Editorial Assistant** | Kate Winzenburg |
| **Writer, Modern Version** | Wim Coleman |
| **Design Director** | Randy Messer |
| **Design** | Mark Hagenberg |
| **Production** | Word Designs |
| **Art Research** | Laura Wells |
| **Cover Art** | Brad Holland |

© 2004 **Perfection Learning© Corporation**
1000 North Second Avenue, P.O. Box 500
Logan, Iowa 51546-0500
Tel: 1-800-831-4190 • Fax: 1-800-543-2745

Printed in the United States of America.

Paperback ISBN 0-7891-6088-9
Cover Craft ISBN 0-7569-1490-6
  2 3 4 5 6  PP  07 06 05 04

# Table of Contents

# Shakespeare's Times: The Gunpowder Plot

Imagine a plot to blow up the Capitol while the President makes a speech to both branches of Congress. Then suppose that the President himself foils the conspiracy. Americans would breathe a huge sigh of relief—but fear of terrorists would linger. According to historian Garry Wills, *Macbeth* was influenced by a similar situation, known as the Gunpowder Plot.

King James I

In 1605, conspirators planned to blow up the English Parliament when all of its members and the royal family were inside.

English Catholics had hoped that King James I, who succeeded the throne in 1603, would remove the ban on practicing their religion. Instead, restrictions on Catholics were tightened. Catholics who refused to attend Church of England services were fined. Skipping church could cost as much as 20 pounds—a whole year's wages for some families. Continued refusal to participate in the official state religion resulted in jail sentences. This ongoing persecution fueled the Gunpowder Plot.

Before this plot could be carried out, a mysterious letter fell into the king's hands. The letter warned its recipient (a member of Parliament) to stay away from the House of Lords on November 5. According to legend, the letter's deeper meaning was revealed to James in a flash of divine inspiration. The would-be assassin, Guy Fawkes, was captured in the cellar below the House of Lords as he waited to ignite a barrel of gunpowder.

As details of the plot were revealed, the whole business seemed increasingly monstrous. For example, the conspirators had participated in a Black Mass (a ceremony used to summon Satan) to ensure the success of their plot. This news intrigued the king, who was fascinated with witchcraft. Like any good politician, King James turned his brush with disaster into a public relations coup. And he was in need of good public

The three Witches

relations. Since James was not comfortable with large crowds, he was not as popular a ruler as his aunt, Queen Elizabeth I.

*Macbeth* makes many flattering references to the king, who was considered a hero for thwarting the conspiracy. The noble Banquo (who historically never existed) is presented as the king's direct ancestor. And in Act IV, King Edward is said to heal people by the touch of his hand—a feat which James I was also reputedly able to perform.

*Macbeth* is clearly one of the most powerful of a group of plays in which Shakespeare explores the nature of evil. In these plays, Shakespeare appears to be seeking some answer to the ancient riddle of why there is so much evil in the world—and why even good people fall prey to it.

# Shakespeare's Sources:
# The Legend of Macbeth

The overwhelming presence of evil in *Macbeth* raises an interesting question: Just how wicked was the historical Macbeth? Shakespeare was not a writer who let facts stand in the way of a good story; the real Macbeth was not the murderous tyrant portrayed in his play.

Vivien Leigh and Laurence Olivier, Stratford-on-Avon, 1955

According to less-biased accounts, Macbeth ruled Scotland wisely and effectively from 1040 to 1057. His people prospered during his reign, and he brought an end to a long conflict between the Scottish Church and the Pope. Macbeth and his wife generously supported monasteries, and he even made a pilgrimage to Rome. Perhaps most significantly, he was the last Scottish king to devote himself to the language and traditions of the Celts, a people who periodically dominated the British Isles throughout antiquity.

Macbeth *did* kill his predecessor Duncan. But he did so in open combat, not while Duncan lay asleep. Moreover, Duncan was not the pious and kind ruler Shakespeare made him out to be. He ruled for only six years, and according to contemporary accounts, he did so very badly. He was cruel and aggressive, involving Scotland in a long war that caused his people great suffering. Perhaps worst of all, he was simply not very capable. When Macbeth defeated Duncan and assumed the throne, the Scottish people rightly expected better times.

Maurice Evans and Judith Anderson in a film of *Macbeth* directed by George Schaefer, 1961

So Shakespeare did with Macbeth as he had already done with Richard III—he took a basically decent ruler and demonized him. But Shakespeare did not create this murderous, tyrannical Macbeth from scratch. Much of the legend had been around for many years. Why and how did it come about?

According to a familiar saying, history is always written by victors. When Macbeth was killed by Malcolm, Duncan's family was permanently restored to the throne. Not surprisingly, this line of royalty was anxious to have its legitimacy honored. Any kind words historians had to say about Macbeth were repressed. Even Shakespeare had political reasons for giving a negative portrayal of Macbeth. King James I traced his lineage back not only to the mythical Banquo but also to Duncan himself.

Three centuries after Macbeth's reign, a historian named Hector Boece described Macbeth as a bloodthirsty monster. This account was largely accepted by Raphael Holinshed in his 1587 book *Chronicles of England, Scotlande, and Ireland*.

Shakespeare used Holinshed's *Chronicles* as a source of information for all his plays dealing with British history, and *Macbeth* was no exception. Holinshed told of the Witches' prophecies and the ascension of Banquo's descendants to the throne of Scotland. But as dramatists will, Shakespeare took liberties with his source. He combined Holinshed's account of Macbeth's rise to power with the story of Donwald, an earlier Scottish tyrant who murdered King Duffe.

There Shakespeare found some of the most gripping elements of his drama. Like Shakespeare's Macbeth, Donwald committed his initial crime by night while the king was a guest in his castle—a violation of the sacred rules of hospitality. Like Macbeth, Donwald was goaded to action by his ambitious and iron-willed wife.

Lady Macbeth and Macbeth at the banquet

However freely Shakespeare may have played with historical facts, he was reasonably faithful to the feudal, Celtic politics of Macbeth's time. Today's audiences may be surprised by Macbeth's alarm in Act I when he hears Duncan declare his own eldest son, Malcolm, the heir to the Scottish throne. We are used to royal succession by primogeniture. This system automatically makes the eldest child (typically a male) the heir to all of a parent's property—including a crown. So why *wouldn't* Malcolm rule after his father's death?

In Scotland, the kingship was *elective*. A group of nobles (called *thanes*) were eligible to rule because they were descendants of Kenneth Mac Alpine. This was the man who, in the 9th century, united Scotland and became its first king. When a king died, a new ruler was elected from among the thanes. This system, while simple, seldom ran smoothly. Rebellion and assassination were common. Few Scottish kings died of old age.

So when Shakespeare's Duncan names Malcolm the Prince of Cumberland, he ignores the normal process of succession. According to both history and legend, Macbeth had a stronger claim to the throne than young Malcolm. Assassination would have been an acceptable means of correcting this wrong—although the deceitful murder in Shakespeare's play would certainly have offended the Celtic warrior spirit.

Shakespeare was also correct in suggesting that an era of Scottish history ended with Macbeth's death. His successor Malcolm III was educated in England and sought military alliances with the English. After England was defeated by Normandy's William the Conqueror in 1066, Malcolm replaced the old Celtic ways with the new Anglo-Norman culture. Eventually, his successors thought of themselves as more French than Celt. And with the ascension of James I to the English throne in 1603, Scotland finally became part of Great Britain.

# Timeline

| | |
|---|---|
| **1564** | Shakespeare is baptized. |
| **1568** | Elizabeth I becomes Queen of England. |
| **1572** | Shakespeare begins grammar school. |
| **1576** | Future King James I is born in Scotland. |
| **1580** | Drake sails around the world. |
| **1582** | Shakespeare marries Anne Hathaway. |
| **1583** | Shakespeare's daughter Susanna is baptized. |
| **1585** | Shakespeare's twins, Judith and Hamnet, are baptized. |
| **1588** | Spanish Armada is defeated. |
| **1590** | Scottish witches plot to assassinate King James VI. |
| **1592–94** | Plague closes all London's theaters. |
| **1594** | *Titus Andronicus* becomes first printed Shakespeare play. |
| **1594** | Shakespeare joins the Lord Chamberlain's Men. |
| **1597** | King James publishes *Daemonologie*, a book on witchcraft. |
| **1599** | Lord Chamberlain's Men build the Globe Theatre; Shakespeare is part-owner of the building. |
| **1603** | March 24: Queen Elizabeth dies childless; King James VI of Scotland becomes King James I of England. |
| **1605** | Gunpowder Plot to blow up Parliament is foiled. |
| **1606** | First recorded performance of *Macbeth* is given at Court. |
| **1609** | Shakespeare's *Sonnets*, written about 1592–1598, published for the first time. |
| **1610** | Shakespeare retires to Stratford. |
| **1613** | Globe Theatre burns to the ground. |
| **1616** | William Shakespeare dies at the age of 52. |
| **1623** | Shakespeare's wife dies. |
| | First Folio published. |

# Reading *Macbeth*

## Using This Parallel Text

This edition of *Macbeth* is especially designed for readers who aren't familiar with Shakespeare. If you're fairly comfortable with his language, simply read the original text on the left-hand page. When you come to a confusing word or passage, refer to the modern English version on the right or the footnotes at the bottom.

If you think Elizabethan English doesn't even sound like English, read a passage of the modern version silently. Then read the same passage of the original. You'll find that Shakespeare's language begins to come alive for you. You may choose to work your way through the entire play this way.

As you read more, you'll probably find yourself using the modern version less and less. Remember, the parallel version is meant to be an aid, not a substitute for the original. If you read only the modern version, you'll cheat yourself out of Shakespeare's language—his quick-witted puns, sharp-tongued insults, and mood-making images.

Keep in mind that language is a living thing, constantly growing and changing. New words are invented and new definitions for old words are added. Since Shakespeare wrote over four hundred years ago, it is not surprising that his work seems challenging to today's readers.

Here are some other reading strategies that can increase your enjoyment of the play.

## Background

Knowing some historical background makes it easier to understand what's going on. In addition to the timeline, you will find information about Shakespeare's life and Elizabethan theater at the back of the book. Reading the summaries that precede each act will also help you to follow the action of the play.

# Getting the Beat

Like most dramatists of his time, Shakespeare frequently used **blank verse** in his plays. In blank verse, the text is written in measured lines that do not rhyme. Look at the following example from *Macbeth*.

> Then live, Macduff: what need I fear of thee?
> But yet I'll make assurance double sure
> And take my bond of fate. Thou shalt not live,
> That I may tell pale-hearted fear it lies . . .

You can see that the four lines above are approximately equal in length, but they do not cover the whole width of the page as the lines in a story or essay might. They are, in fact, unrhymed verse with each line containing ten or eleven syllables. Furthermore, the ten syllables can be divided into five sections, called **iambs**, or feet. Each iamb contains one unstressed (**U**) and one stressed (**/**) syllable. Try reading the lines below, giving emphasis to the capitalized syllable in each iamb.

| U / | U / | U / | U / | U / |
|---|---|---|---|---|
| Then LIVE | MacDUFF | what NEED | I FEAR | of THEE? |

| U / | U / | U / | U / | U / |
|---|---|---|---|---|
| But YET | I'll MAKE | asSUR | ance DOU | ble SURE . . . |

The length of a line of verse is measured by counting the stresses. This length is known as the **meter**, and when there are five stresses and the rhythm follows an unstressed/stressed pattern, it is known as **iambic pentameter**. Much of Shakespeare's work is written in iambic pentameter.

Of course, Shakespeare was not rigid about this format. He sometimes varied the lines by putting accents in unusual places, by having lines with more or fewer than ten syllables, and by varying where pauses occur. An actor's interpretation can also add variety. (Only a terrible actor would deliver lines in a way that makes the rhythm sound singsong!)

Macbeth's castle,
Dunsinane, in an
Orson Welles film,
1948

## Prose

In addition to verse, Shakespeare wrote speeches in **prose**, or language without rhythmic structure. Look at the Porter's speech on pages 86–88. If you try beating out an iambic rhythm to these lines, you'll discover that it doesn't work because they're in prose. But once Macbeth enters and starts speaking, you'll be able to find the rhythm of iambic pentameter again. Shakespeare often uses prose for comic speeches, to show madness, and for characters of lower social rank such as servants. His upper-class characters generally do not speak in prose. But these weren't hard and fast rules as far as Shakespeare was concerned. Whether characters speak in verse or prose is often a function of the situation and who they're addressing, as well as their social status.

## Contractions

As you know, contractions are words that have been combined by substituting an apostrophe for a letter or letters that have been removed. Contractions were as common in Shakespeare's time as they are today. For example, we use *it's* as a contraction for the words *it is*. In Shakespeare's writing you will discover that *'tis* means the same thing. Shakespeare often used the apostrophe to shorten words so that they would fit into the rhythmic pattern of a line. This is especially true of verbs ending in *-ed*. Note that in Shakespeare's plays, the *-ed* at the end of a verb is usually pronounced as a separate syllable. Therefore, *walked* would be pronounced as two syllables, *walk\*ed*, while *walk'd* would be only one.

## Speak and Listen

Remember that plays are written to be acted, not read silently. Reading out loud—whether in a group or alone—helps you to "hear" the meaning. Listening to another reader will also help. You might also enjoy listening to a recording of the play by professional actors.

## Clues and Cues

Shakespeare was sparing in his use of stage directions. In fact, many of those in modern editions were added by later editors. Added stage directions are usually indicated by brackets. For example, [*aside*] tells the actor to give the audience information that the other characters can't hear.

Sometimes a character's actions are suggested by the lines themselves. When Macbeth's dinner guests ask him to sit down in Act III, Scene iv, Macbeth replies, "The table's full." This tells us that Macbeth is looking at the back of his own chair, for he sees a figure in the chair but doesn't recognize it as Banquo's ghost. Macbeth must walk in front of the chair before he exclaims, "Which of you have done this?"

## The Play's the Thing

Finally, if you can't figure out every word in the play, don't get discouraged. The people in Shakespeare's audience couldn't either. At that time, language was changing rapidly and standardized spelling, punctuation, grammar, and even dictionaries did not exist. Besides, Shakespeare loved to play with words. He made up new combinations, like *fat-guts* and *mumble-news*. To make matters worse, the actors probably spoke very rapidly. But the audience didn't strain to catch every word. They went to a Shakespeare play for the same reasons we go to a movie—to get caught up in the story and the acting, to have a great laugh, or a good cry.

# Cast of Characters

**DUNCAN** King of Scotland
**MALCOLM** his elder son
**DONALBAIN** Duncan's younger son
**CAPTAIN** in the King's army
**MACBETH** Thane of Glamis, then Thane of Cawdor, then King of Scotland
**SEYTON** his armor bearer
**LADY MACBETH** wife of Macbeth
**A GENTLEWOMAN** servant to Lady Macbeth
**PORTER** servant at Macbeth's castle
**BANQUO** a Thane (nobleman of Scotland)
**FLEANCE** his son
**MACDUFF** Thane of Fife
**LADY MACDUFF** wife of Macduff
**SON** to the Macduffs
**LENNOX**
**ROSS**
**MENTEITH** } other Thanes
**ANGUS**
**CAITHNESS**
**A DOCTOR**
**AN OLD MAN**
**THREE MURDERERS**
**LORDS, SOLDIERS, SERVANTS, MESSENGERS**

## In England

**SIWARD** Earl of Northumberland
**YOUNG SIWARD** his son
**DOCTOR**

## From the Supernatural World

**WITCHES**
**HECATE**
**APPARITIONS**

**TIME** the 11th century

**PLACE** Scotland and England

# Macbeth

## ACT I

Orson Welles in his 1948 film of *Macbeth*

"Fair is foul,
and foul is fair."

# Before You Read

1. This play opens with three witches making plans to meet Macbeth. What kind of play do you expect after such an opening scene?

2. The Witches make prophecies to Macbeth and Banquo. How would you react to someone who promised to reveal your own future?

3. Consider what you learn about Macbeth in the first scenes.

4. As you read, think about how others' views of the Macbeths compare to the way they really are.

# Literary Elements

1. **Imagery** refers to words that appeal to the five senses: hearing, taste, touch, sight, and sound. Such word pictures can suggest a mood or idea, and they add emotion and power to the writing. In Act I, Scene iii, Macbeth says, "Why do you dress me / In borrow'd robes?" This is the first of many images of borrowed or ill-fitting clothing in *Macbeth*. They contribute to the ideas that Macbeth is not the natural king of Scotland, and he feels insecure in this role.

2. A **simile** is a way of comparing two unlike things using *like* or *as*. In the play, Lady Macbeth says, "The sleeping and the dead / Are but as pictures." If the sleeping and the dead are like paintings—still and not alive—Macbeth need not fear murdering the sleeping Duncan.

3. **Soliloquies** are longer speeches that allow characters to reveal their innermost thoughts and feelings to the audience. In Act I, Scene v, Lady Macbeth has a soliloquy ("Glamis thou art . . ."), in which she questions whether Macbeth has what it takes to kill King Duncan. She believes Macbeth's nature "is too full o' the milk o' human kindness."

4. A **euphemism** is an indirect way of expressing something; it may be more polite—or less harsh—than the reality. In Act II, Scene ii, Lady Macbeth says, "Had he not resembled / My father as he slept, I had done 't." "Had done 't" is less brutal than saying "had murdered Duncan."

# Words to Know

The following vocabulary words appear in Act I in the original text of Shakespeare's play. However, they are words that are still commonly used. Read the definitions here and pay attention to the words as you read the play (they will be in boldfaced type).

| | |
|---|---|
| **chastise** | scold; punish |
| **corporal** | physical; bodily |
| **disdaining** | ridiculing; showing contempt for |
| **harbinger** | warning; signal |
| **impedes** | prevents; hinders |
| **implored** | begged; beseeched |
| **peerless** | unique; matchless |
| **procreant** | fertile; fruitful |
| **prophetic** | making a prediction |
| **rapt** | absorbed; engrossed |
| **recompense** | payment; retribution |
| **repentance** | sorrow; remorse |
| **soliciting** | selling; persuading |
| **surmise** | guess; suppose |

# Act Summary

Scotland is at war!

King Duncan of Scotland is faced with an invading army from Norway and also rebellious subjects at home. Fortunately, he's got a valiant nobleman among his ranks—Macbeth, the Thane of Glamis. Helped by his friend Banquo, Macbeth leads Duncan's forces to victory.

The play begins after the battle, when Macbeth and Banquo meet the three Witches, who greet Macbeth by his title, the Thane of Glamis. But they predict that he will soon be Thane of Cawdor—and later King of Scotland. As for Banquo, the Witches promise that he will be the father of kings, even though he'll never be king himself.

The Witches disappear without telling them more.

The Witches, Orson Welles film, 1948

Then a messenger arrives, bringing Macbeth and Banquo amazing news. The traitorous Thane of Cawdor is about to be executed. King Duncan has declared Macbeth the new Thane of Cawdor. The Witches' first prediction has come true.

To celebrate the victory, King Duncan decides to visit Macbeth's castle in Inverness. Macbeth arrives at Inverness ahead of the King. He and his wife, Lady Macbeth, talk about the Witches' prophecies.

Lady Macbeth urges Macbeth to kill Duncan during his visit. Reluctant at first, Macbeth gives in.

# ACT I, SCENE I

*[An open place.] Thunder and lightning. Enter three*
WITCHES.

**FIRST WITCH**
When shall we three meet again
In thunder, lightning, or in rain?

**SECOND WITCH**
When the hurlyburly's done,
When the battle's lost and won.

**THIRD WITCH**
5    That will be ere the set of sun.

**FIRST WITCH**
Where the place?

**SECOND WITCH**
                    Upon the heath.*

**THIRD WITCH**
There to meet with Macbeth.

**FIRST WITCH**
I come, Graymalkin!*

**SECOND WITCH**
10    Paddock* calls.

**THIRD WITCH**
Anon.

**ALL**
Fair is foul, and foul is fair.
Hover through the fog and filthy air.

*Exeunt.*

---

7    *heath*  barren, open country, covered with small shrubs

9    *Graymalkin*  gray cat. This is the "familiar," or attendant spirit, of the First Witch.

10    *Paddock*  a toad. It is the "familiar" of the Second Witch.

# ACT 1, SCENE 1

*Scotland. An open place. Thunder and lightning.*
*Three* WITCHES *enter.*

**FIRST WITCH**
When shall we three meet again?
In thunder, lightning, or in rain?

**SECOND WITCH**
When the uproar is all over,
and the battle's been lost and won.

**THIRD WITCH**
That will be before sunset.                                     5

**FIRST WITCH**
Where will we meet?

**SECOND WITCH**
Upon the heath.

**THIRD WITCH**
There we will meet with Macbeth.

**FIRST WITCH**
I come, Graymalkin!

**SECOND WITCH**
Paddock calls for me.                                          10

**THIRD WITCH**
Quickly!

**ALL**
Pleasant is foul, and foul is pleasant;
Let's hover through the fog and filthy air.

*They exit.*

# ACT I, SCENE II

[*A military camp.*] *Alarum within. Enter* DUNCAN, MALCOLM, DONALBAIN, LENNOX, *with* ATTENDANTS, *meeting a bleeding* CAPTAIN.

**DUNCAN**
What bloody man is that? He can report,
As seemeth by his plight, of the revolt
The newest state.

**MALCOLM**
               This is the sergeant*
5    Who like a good and hardy soldier fought
'Gainst my captivity. Hail, brave friend!
Say to the King the knowledge of the broil
As thou didst leave it.

**CAPTAIN**
               Doubtful it stood,
10  As two spent swimmers, that do cling together
And choke their art. The merciless Macdonwald—
Worthy to be a rebel, for to that
The multiplying villainies of nature
Do swarm upon him—from the Western Isles
15  Of kerns and gallowglasses is supplied;
And Fortune,* on his damned quarrel smiling,
Show'd like a rebel's whore: but all's too weak:
For brave Macbeth—well he deserves that name—
**Disdaining** Fortune, with his brandish'd steel,
20  Which smoked with bloody execution,
Like valor's minion carved out his passage
Till he faced the slave;
Which ne'er shook hands, nor bade farewell to him,
Till he unseam'd him from the nave to th' chops,
25  And fix'd his head upon our battlements.

**DUNCAN**
O valiant cousin! Worthy gentleman!

---

4   *sergeant* a much higher rank than a modern sergeant. He was probably a knight or squire and thus could be called "Captain" in the stage directions.

16  *Fortune* the personified power that determines human success, distributing

# ACT 1, SCENE 2

*A camp near Forres. Trumpet call offstage.* DUNCAN,
MALCOLM, DONALBAIN, LENNOX, *and* SERVANTS *enter. They
meet a bleeding* CAPTAIN.

**DUNCAN**
Who is that bloody man? Judging from his troubles,
he can report to us† the latest news
of the revolt.

**MALCOLM**
This is the sergeant
who fought like a good and hardy soldier                                    5
to save me from captivity. Greetings, brave friend!
Tell the King all you know of the fighting
when you left it.

**CAPTAIN**
The outcome was hard to guess,
just as when two tired swimmers cling together                              10
and pull each other down. The merciless Macdonwald
is worthy to be a rebel; and for that reason,
countless villains from all over the world
swarm around him like insects. He's aided
by kerns and gallowglasses from the Hebrides,                               15
and Fortune smiled on his cursed cause—
falsely, like a rebel's whore. But all was in vain,
for brave Macbeth (he deserves that name well)
scorned Fortune with his swinging sword,
which steamed with the blood of the slain.                                  20
Like valor's favorite, he slashed his way
until he faced the villain.
Without bothering to shake hands with him, or to say farewell,
he ripped him open from his navel to his jaws
and stuck his head on our battlements.                                      25

**DUNCAN**
Oh valiant cousin, worthy gentleman!

---

happiness and unhappiness according to her own whims, showing some favor to
all men but being constant to none

†   *to us* Duncan is using the royal "we."

**CAPTAIN**

As whence the sun 'gins his reflection
Shipwracking storms and direful thunders break,
So from that spring whence comfort seemed to come
30    Discomfort swells. Mark, King of Scotland, mark:
No sooner justice had,with valour arm'd
Compell'd these skipping kerns to trust their heels,
But the Norweyan lord, surveying vantage,
With furbish'd arms and new supplies of men,
35    Began a fresh assault.

**DUNCAN**

Dismayed not this
Our captains, Macbeth and Banquo?

**CAPTAIN**

Yes,
As sparrows eagles, or the hare the lion.
40    If I say sooth, I must report they were
As cannons overcharged with double cracks,
So they doubly redoubled strokes upon the foe.
Except they meant to bathe in reeking wounds,
Or memorise another Golgotha,*
45    I cannot tell—
But I am faint, my gashes cry for help.

**DUNCAN**

So well thy words become thee as thy wounds;
They smack of honour both. Go get him surgeons.

[*Exit* CAPTAIN, *attended.*]

*Enter* ROSS *and* ANGUS.

Who comes here?

**MALCOLM**

50                              The worthy Thane of Ross.

**LENNOX**

What a haste looks through his eyes! So should he look
That seems to speak things strange.

---

44    *Golgotha* Calvary, the "place of skulls" where Christ was crucified

**CAPTAIN**

Shipwrecking storms and grim thunderbolts often come
from the east, where the sun rises;
in just such a way, new disasters fell upon us
from what had seemed the source of our comfort. Listen, King     30
   of Scotland, listen:
No sooner had justice, armed with valor,
forced these nimble kerns to take to their heels,
but the King of Norway saw a new opportunity.
With brightly polished arms and new supplies of men,
he started a fresh attack.     35

**DUNCAN**

Didn't this disturb
our captains, Macbeth and Banquo?

**CAPTAIN**

Yes,
like sparrows disturb eagles, or the hare the lion.
To tell the truth, I must report that they were     40
like cannons overloaded with two cannonballs each;
they doubled, then doubled again, their strokes against the foe.
Whether they meant to bathe in bloody wounds,
or cause the battlefield to be remembered like another Golgotha,
I cannot say —     45
But I am faint; my wounds cry out for help.

**DUNCAN**

Your words suit you well, just like your wounds:
they both taste like honor. Go get him doctors.

   *The* CAPTAIN *is led away.*

   ROSS *and* ANGUS *enter.*

Who comes here?

**MALCOLM**

The worthy Thane of Ross.     50

**LENNOX**

What haste can be seen in his eyes! That's how a man would look
if he were about to say strange things.

**ROSS**

God save the King!

**DUNCAN**

Whence cam'st thou, worthy thane?

**ROSS**

55 From Fife, great King;
Where the Norweyan banners flout the sky
And fan our people cold.
Norway himself, with terrible numbers,
Assisted by that most disloyal traitor
60 The Thane of Cawdor, began a dismal conflict;
Till that Bellona's* bridegroom, lapped in proof,
Confronted him with self-comparisons,
Point against point, rebellious arm 'gainst arm,
Curbing his lavish spirit; and, to conclude,
65 The victory fell on us.

**DUNCAN**

Great happiness!

**ROSS**

That now, Sweno,
The Norways' king, craves composition;
Nor would we deign him burial of his men
70 Till he disbursed at Saint Colme's Inch*
Ten thousand dollars* to our general use.

**DUNCAN**

No more that Thane of Cawdor shall deceive
Our bosom interest. Go pronounce his present death,
And with his former title greet Macbeth.

**ROSS**

75 I'll see it done.

**DUNCAN**

What he hath lost, noble Macbeth hath won.

*Exeunt.*

---

61  *Bellona*  In Roman mythology, the sister of the God of War, Mars

70  *Saint Colme's Inch*  St. Columba's Island, Inchcolm, near Edinburgh

71  *dollars*  English for the German Thaler, a silver coin well known to the Elizabethans. It is an anachronism here, since the coin was first minted in the sixteenth century and Macbeth takes place in the eleventh century.

**ROSS**

God save the King.

**DUNCAN**

Where did you come from, worthy thane?

**ROSS**

From Fife, great King, 55
where the Norwegian banners defy the sky
and chill our people with fear.
The King of Norway himself started a fearful battle
with a huge number of soldiers—helped out
by that most disloyal traitor, the Thane of Cawdor. 60
But then came Macbeth, the war-goddess's husband, dressed in
    mighty armor,
he faced the king with equal skill and courage—
sword against sword, arm against rebellious arm,
taming his undisciplined spirit. To conclude, the victory fell to us. 65

**DUNCAN**

Great happiness!

**ROSS**

And now
Sweno, Norway's king, wants to make peace.
We wouldn't allow him to bury his men
until he gave ten thousand dollars for our general use 70
at Saint Colme's Inch.

**DUNCAN**

Never again will that Thane of Cawdor deceive
my trusting heart. Go command his immediate execution,
and greet Macbeth with his former title.

**ROSS**

I'll take care of it. 75

**DUNCAN**

What he has lost, noble Macbeth has won.

>       *They exit.*

# ACT I, SCENE III

*[A heath.] Thunder. Enter the three* WITCHES.

**FIRST WITCH**
Where hast thou been, sister?

**SECOND WITCH**
Killing swine.

**THIRD WITCH**
Sister, where thou?

**FIRST WITCH**
A sailor's wife had chestnuts in her lap,
5 And mounched, and mounched, and mounched.
"Give me," quoth I.
"Aroint thee, witch!" the rump-fed ronyon* cries.
Her husband's to Aleppo gone, master o' th' *Tiger:* *
But in a sieve I'll thither sail,
10 And, like a rat without a tail,
I'll do, I'll do, and I'll do.

**SECOND WITCH**
I'll give thee a wind.

**FIRST WITCH**
Th' art kind.

**THIRD WITCH**
And I another.

**FIRST WITCH**
15 I myself have all the other,
And the very ports they blow,
All the quarters that they know
I' th' shipman's card.
I'll drain him dry as hay:
20 Sleep shall neither night nor day
Hang upon his penthouse lid;
He shall live a man forbid:
Weary sev'nnights nine times nine

---

7  *ronyon*  a mangy or scabby creature, usually used as a general term of contempt

8  *Tiger*  the name of the ship making the journey to Aleppo, a city in northern Syria

# ACT 1, SCENE 3

*A heath near Forres. Thunder. The three* WITCHES *enter.*

**FIRST WITCH**
Where have you been, sister?

**SECOND WITCH**
Killing swine.

**THIRD WITCH**
Sister, where were you?

**FIRST WITCH**
A sailor's wife had chestnuts in her lap,
and munched, and munched, and munched.                                    5
"Give me some," I said.
"Begone, witch!" the fat-rumped, scabby woman cried.
Her husband has gone to Aleppo—the master of the Tiger.
But I'll sail there in a sieve,
and in the shape of a tailless rat,                                       10
I'll do him in, I'll do him in, I'll do him in.

**SECOND WITCH**
I'll give you a wind.

**FIRST WITCH**
You are kind.

**THIRD WITCH**
And I'll give another.

**FIRST WITCH**
I myself have all the other winds;                                        15
they blow away from every port,
and they know all the directions
in the navigator's compass.
I will drain him as dry as hay:
sleep will hang upon his eyelids                                          20
neither night nor day;
he will live a cursed man.
For nine times nine weary weeks,

Shall he dwindle, peak and pine.
25 Though his bark cannot be lost,
Yet it shall be tempest-tost.
Look what I have.

**SECOND WITCH**
Show me, show me.

**FIRST WITCH**
Here I have a pilot's thumb,
30 Wrack'd as homeward he did come.

*Drum within.*

**THIRD WITCH**
A drum, a drum!
Macbeth doth come.

**ALL** [*dancing in a circle*]
The Weïrd* Sisters, hand in hand,
Posters of the sea and land,
35 Thus do go about, about:
Thrice to thine and thrice to mine
And thrice again, to make up nine.
Peace! The charm's wound up.

*Enter* MACBETH *and* BANQUO.

**MACBETH**
So foul and fair a day I have not seen.

**BANQUO**
40 How far is 't called to Forres?* What are these
So withered and so wild in their attire,
That look not like th' inhabitants o' th' earth,
And yet are on 't? Live you, or are you aught
That man may question? You seem to understand me,
45 By each at once her choppy finger laying
Upon her skinny lips. You should be women,
And yet your beards forbid me to interpret
That you are so.

---

33  *weïrd* from the Old English "wyrd," meaning fate or destiny

40  *Forres* a town in northern Scotland, to the south of Moray Firth, between Elgin and Nairn

he will dwindle, hunger, and waste away.
Though his ship cannot be lost,                                    25
it will still be tossed by tempests.
Look at what I have.

**SECOND WITCH**
Show me, show me.

**FIRST WITCH**
Here I have the thumb of a pilot
wrecked when he was coming home.                                   30

> *Drum offstage.*

**THIRD WITCH**
A drum, a drum!
Macbeth is coming.

**ALL** (*dancing in a circle*)
The Weïrd Sisters, hand in hand,
swift travelers over the sea and land,
this way go around and around—                                     35
three times for you, three times for me
and three times again, to make up nine.
Now be quiet! The spell is ready.

> MACBETH *and* BANQUO *enter.*

**MACBETH**
I've never seen a day both so foul and pleasant.

**BANQUO**
How far do you think it is to Forres? Who are these creatures,     40
so withered and wild in their clothing
that they don't look like inhabitants of the earth,
even though they are on it? Are you alive? Are you anything
that a man can put questions to? You seem to understand me,
because each of you puts a chapped finger                          45
against her skinny lips. You must surely be women,
and yet your beards will not allow me
to call you women.

**MACBETH**

                      Speak, if you can. What are you?

**FIRST WITCH**

50     All hail, Macbeth! Hail to thee, Thane of Glamis!*

**SECOND WITCH**

     All hail, Macbeth! Hail to thee, Thane of Cawdor!*

**THIRD WITCH**

     All hail, Macbeth, that shalt be King hereafter!

**BANQUO**

     Good sir, why do you start and seem to fear
     Things that do sound so fair?—I' th' name of truth,
55     Are ye fantastical, or that indeed
     Which outwardly ye show? My noble partner
     You greet with present grace and great prediction
     Of noble having and of royal hope,
     That he seems rapt withal: to me you speak not.
60     If you can look into the seeds of time,
     And say which grain will grow and which will not,
     Speak then to me, who neither beg nor fear
     Your favors nor your hate.

**FIRST WITCH**

     Hail!

**SECOND WITCH**

65     Hail!

**THIRD WITCH**

     Hail!

**FIRST WITCH**

     Lesser than Macbeth, and greater.

**SECOND WITCH**

     Not so happy, yet much happier.

**THIRD WITCH**

     Thou shalt get kings, though thou be none.
70     So all hail, Macbeth and Banquo!

---

50   *Glamis*  a castle and village north of Dundee, near the modern town of Forfar

51   *Cawdor*  located in northwestern Nairnshire, between Inverness and Forres

**MACBETH**

Speak if you can. Who are you?

**FIRST WITCH**

All hail, Macbeth! Hail to you, Thane of Glamis!                    50

**SECOND WITCH**

All hail, Macbeth! Hail to you, Thane of Cawdor!

**THIRD WITCH**

All hail, Macbeth, who will be King later on!

**BANQUO** (*to* MACBETH)

Good sir, why are you so startled, seeming to fear
things that sound so pleasant? (*to the* WITCHES) In the name of
    truth, are you imaginary, or are you really                    55
what you outwardly appear to be? You greet
my noble partner with both his present title and a prediction of
    further greatness—
of a nobleman's possessions and the hope of becoming a king;
he seems completely entranced. But to me, you say nothing.
If you can look into the seeds of time                    60
and say which grain will grow and which will not,
then speak to me, for I neither beg
your favors nor fear your hate.

**FIRST WITCH**

Hail!

**SECOND WITCH**

Hail!                    65

**THIRD WITCH**

Hail!

**FIRST WITCH**

Lesser than Macbeth, and greater.

**SECOND WITCH**

Not so happy, and yet much happier.

**THIRD WITCH**

You will be a father to kings, even though you won't be a king
    yourself.
So all hail, Macbeth and Banquo!                    70

**FIRST WITCH**

Banquo and Macbeth, all hail!

**MACBETH**

Stay, you imperfect speakers, tell me more.
By Sinel's death I know I am Thane of Glamis;
But how of Cawdor? The Thane of Cawdor lives,
75    A prosperous gentleman; and to be King
Stands not within the prospect of belief,
No more than to be Cawdor. Say from whence
You owe this strange intelligence? Or why
Upon this blasted heath you stop our way
80    With such **prophetic** greeting? Speak, I charge you.

        WITCHES *vanish.*

**BANQUO**

The earth hath bubbles as the water has,
And these are of them. Whither are they vanished?

**MACBETH**

Into the air; and what seemed **corporal** melted
As breath into the wind. Would they had stay'd!

**BANQUO**

85    Were such things here as we do speak about?
Or have we eaten on the insane root*
That takes the reason prisoner?

**MACBETH**

Your children shall be kings.

**BANQUO**

                      You shall be King.

**MACBETH**

90    And Thane of Cawdor too. Went it not so?

**BANQUO**

To th' selfsame tune and words.—Who's here?

        *Enter* ROSS *and* ANGUS.

**ROSS**

The King hath happily received, Macbeth,

---

86   *insane root* an herb or root causing insanity. Shakespeare may have had in mind
such plants as hemlock, henbane, or deadly nightshade.

**FIRST WITCH**
>Banquo and Macbeth, all hail!

**MACBETH**
>Stay, you incomplete speakers, and tell me more.
>By Sinel's death, I know I am Thane of Glamis;
>but how can I be Thane of Cawdor? The Thane of Cawdor lives—
>a prosperous gentleman. And to be King                75
>is no more to be believed
>than to be Thane of Cawdor. Tell me—where
>did you get this strange information? And why
>do you stop us on our way across this barren heath
>with such a prophetic greeting? Speak, I command you.        80

>>*The* WITCHES *vanish.*

**BANQUO**
>The earth has bubbles, just like water has—
>and these creatures are made of them. Where have they vanished?

**MACBETH**
>Into the air—and what seemed solid has melted,
>like breath into the wind. I wish they had stayed!

**BANQUO**
>Were these things we speak about really here?        85
>Or have we eaten from a root that causes insanity
>and takes the reason prisoner?

**MACBETH**
>Your children will be kings.

**BANQUO**
>You will be king.

**MACBETH**
>And Thane of Cawdor, too. Isn't that how it went?        90

**BANQUO**
>To the very same tune and words.—Who's here?

>>ROSS *and* ANGUS *enter.*

**ROSS**
>Macbeth, the King has happily received

The news of thy success; and when he reads
Thy personal venture in the rebels' fight,
95  His wonders and his praises do contend
Which should be thine or his. Silenced with that,
In viewing o'er the rest o' th' selfsame day,
He finds thee in the stout Norweyan ranks,
Nothing afeard of what thyself didst make,
100  Strange images of death. As thick as hail
Came post with post; and every one did bear
Thy praises in his kingdom's great defence,
And pour'd them down before him.

**ANGUS**

                                    We are sent
105  To give thee, from our royal master, thanks;
Only to herald thee into his sight,
Not pay thee.

**ROSS**

And for an earnest of a greater honour,
He bade me, from him, call thee Thane of Cawdor,
110  In which addition, hail, most worthy Thane!
For it is thine.

**BANQUO**

                    What, can the devil speak true?

**MACBETH**

The Thane of Cawdor lives: why do you dress me
In borrow'd robes?

**ANGUS**

                              Who was the Thane lives yet,
115  But under heavy judgment bears that life
Which he deserves to lose. Whether he was combined
With those of Norway, or did line the rebel
With hidden help and vantage, or that with both
120  He laboured in his country's wrack, I know not;
But treasons capital, confessed and proved,
Have overthrown him.

the news of your successes; when he considered
your personal boldness while fighting against the rebels,
his astonishment and his praises struggled with one another,    95
and he didn't know whether to express his feelings or keep
    them to himself. He viewed
your deeds for the rest of the day in silence,
and found you in the strong Norwegian ranks,
not at all frightened by what you made yourself—
strange pictures of death. As thick as hail                     100
came messenger after messenger, and every one brought
praises for your great defense of his kingdom,
and poured those praises down before him.

**ANGUS**

We've been sent
by our royal master to give you thanks—                         105
but only to announce you into his presence,
and not to pay you.

**ROSS**

And as a pledge of a greater honor,
he asked me, on his behalf, to call you Thane of Cawdor.
So by that title I say—Hail, most worthy Thane!                 110
For that rank is yours.

**BANQUO**

What, can the devil tell the truth?

**MACBETH**

The Thane of Cawdor lives. Why do you dress me
in borrowed robes?

**ANGUS**

The man who was the Thane still lives—                          115
but under a heavy judgment, he holds onto a life
that he deserves to lose. I do not know
whether he was allied with the Norwegians,
or supported the rebels with secret help and advantages,
or tried to wreck his country by serving them both.            120
But he has overthrown himself by capital treasons
that are confessed and proven.

**MACBETH** [*aside*]

Glamis and Thane of Cawdor!

The greatest is behind. [*to* ROSS *and* ANGUS] Thanks

125     for your pains. [*aside to* BANQUO] Do you not hope your
children shall be kings,

When those that gave the Thane of Cawdor to me

Promised no less to them?

**BANQUO** [*aside to* MACBETH]

                That, trusted home,

130     Might yet enkindle you unto the crown,

Besides the Thane of Cawdor. But 'tis strange:

And oftentimes, to win us to our harm,

The instruments of darkness tell us truths,

Win us with honest trifles, to betray's

135     In deepest consequence.—

Cousins, a word, I pray you.

**MACBETH** [*aside*]

             Two truths are told,

As happy prologues to the swelling act

Of the imperial theme.—I thank you, gentlemen.—

140     [*aside*] This supernatural **soliciting**

Cannot be ill, cannot be good. If ill,

Why hath it given me earnest of success,

Commencing in a truth? I am Thane of Cawdor:

If good, why do I yield to that suggestion

145     Whose horrid image doth unfix my hair

And make my seated heart knock at my ribs,

Against the use of nature? Present fears

Are less than horrible imaginings.

My thought, whose murder yet is but fantastical,

150     Shakes so my single state of man

That function is smothered in **surmise**,

And nothing is but what is not.

**BANQUO**

          Look, how our partner's **rapt**.

**MACBETH** (*aside*)

Glamis, and Thane of Cawdor—
the greatest prophecy is to follow. (*to* ROSS *and* ANGUS)
Thanks for your trouble. (*to* BANQUO) Don't you hope your      125
  children will be kings, since those that gave me the title of
Thane of Cawdor promised no less to them?

**BANQUO** (*to* MACBETH)

If you trust to that completely,
you might start yearning for the crown,      130
besides being Thane of Cawdor. But this is strange.
And oftentimes, to catch us in our own trap,
the instruments of darkness tell us true things,
gaining our confidence with honest trifles, only to betray us
in matters of serious importance.—      135
(*to* ROSS *and* ANGUS) Fellow noblemen, I'd like a word with you.

**MACBETH** (*aside*)

Two fortunate prophecies have proven true
in the beginning to a splendid play
on the theme of kingly power. (*to* ROSS *and* ANGUS) I thank you,
    gentlemen.
(*aside*) This invitation by supernatural beings      140
cannot be bad, and yet it cannot be good. If it is bad,
why has it given me a promise of success,
beginning with something true? I am Thane of Cawdor.
But if it is good, why am I ready to yield to that temptation—
the horrid image of which makes my hair stand on end,      145
and causes my well-fastened heart to beat against my ribs
in such an unnatural way? Frightful things that are actually present
affect one less than imagined horrors.
My murderous thought is still only imaginary,
but it shakes my entire manhood so deeply      150
that my power to act is smothered by expectation,
and nothing seems real except what I imagine.

**BANQUO** (*to* ROSS *and* ANGUS)

Look at how entranced our companion is.

**MACBETH** [*aside*]
  If chance will have me King, why, chance may crown me,
155  Without my stir.

**BANQUO**
                              New horrors come upon him,
  Like our strange garments, cleave not to their mold
  But with the aid of use.

**MACBETH** [*aside*]
                              Come what come may,
160  Time and the hour runs through the roughest day.

**BANQUO**
  Worthy Macbeth, we stay upon your leisure.

**MACBETH**
  Give me your favour. My dull brain was wrought
  With things forgotten. Kind gentlemen, your pains
  Are registered where every day I turn
165  The leaf to read them. Let us toward the King.
  [*aside to* BANQUO] Think upon what hath chanced,
      and at more time,
  The interim having weighed it, let us speak
  Our free hearts each to other.

**BANQUO**
170  Very gladly.

**MACBETH**
  Till then, enough.—Come, friends.

      *Exeunt.*

**MACBETH** (*aside*)
If chance would make me a king, why, chance might crown me
without my doing a thing. 155

**BANQUO** (*to* ROSS *and* ANGUS)
These new honors that have come upon him
are like our new clothes; they will not fit the body's shape
until they've been worn awhile.

**MACBETH** (*aside*)
Whatever should happen,
time will see even the stormiest day to its end. 160

**BANQUO**
Worthy Macbeth, we're waiting until you're ready.

**MACBETH**
I beg your pardon. My dull brain is trying to recall
something I've forgotten. Kind gentlemen, I've written down
your courtesies in my mind, and I'll turn
to that page daily to read about them. Let us go to the King. 165
(*aside to* BANQUO) Think about what has happened, and when we
    have more time,
and have thought it over awhile, let us speak
our hearts freely to each to other.

**BANQUO**
Very gladly. 170

**MACBETH**
That's enough until then.—Come on, friends.

> *They exit.*

# ACT I, SCENE IV

[*Forres. The castle.*] *Flourish. Enter* DUNCAN, LENNOX, MALCOLM, DONALBAIN, *and* ATTENDANTS.

**DUNCAN**

Is execution done on Cawdor? Are not
Those in commission yet returned?

**MALCOLM**

My liege,
They are not yet come back. But I have spoke
5    With one that saw him die: who did report
That very frankly he confessed his treasons,
**Implored** your Highness's pardon and set forth
A deep **repentance**. Nothing in his life
Became him like the leaving it. He died
10    As one that had been studied in his death
To throw away the dearest thing he owed,
As 'twere a careless trifle.

**DUNCAN**

There's no art
To find the mind's construction in the face.
15    He was a gentleman on whom I built
An absolute trust.

*Enter* MACBETH, BANQUO, ROSS, *and* ANGUS.

O worthiest cousin!
The sin of my ingratitude even now
Was heavy on me. Thou art so far before
20    That swiftest wing of **recompense** is slow
To overtake thee. Would thou hadst less deserved,
That the proportion both of thanks and payment
Might have been mine! Only I have left to say,
More is thy due than more than all can pay.

**MACBETH**

25    The service and the loyalty I owe,
In doing it, pays itself. Your Highness's part
Is to receive our duties; and our duties

# ACT 1, SCENE 4

*Forres. A room in the palace. Fanfare.* DUNCAN, LENNOX,
MALCOLM, DONALBAIN, *and* SERVANTS *enter.*

**DUNCAN**

Has the Thane of Cawdor been executed? Haven't
the men assigned to oversee the execution returned yet?

**MALCOLM**

My lord,
they have not yet come back. But I have spoken
with someone who saw him die, who reported          5
that he confessed his treasons very openly,
begged your Highness' pardon, and spoke
with deep repentance. Nothing he did in his life
suited him better than how he left it. He died
like someone who had rehearsed his death,           10
so he could throw away the dearest thing he owned—his life—
as if it were a thing of no importance.

**DUNCAN**

There's no way
to read a person's mind by his face.
He was a gentleman I had learned                     15
to trust completely.

　　　MACBETH, BANQUO, ROSS, *and* ANGUS *enter.*

(*to* MACBETH) Oh worthiest cousin!
I was just now feeling guilty
for my sinful ingratitude. Your achievements come so quickly that,
no matter how quickly I try to pay you back,         20
I can't overtake you. I wish you weren't so deserving,
so you might be in debt to me, instead,
for my payment and thanks! All I can say is
that everything I have to give is not enough to repay you.

**MACBETH**

Just giving the service and loyalty that I owe you   25
is its own reward. It is Your Highness's role
to receive what we owe you; our duties

Are to your throne and state children and servants;
Which do but what they should, by doing every thing

30    Safe toward your love and honour.

**DUNCAN**
                              Welcome hither.
I have begun to plant thee and will labour
To make thee full of growing.—Noble Banquo,
That hast no less deserved, nor must be known

35    No less to have done so, let me enfold thee
And hold thee to my heart.

**BANQUO**
                              There if I grow,
The harvest is your own.

**DUNCAN**
                              My plenteous joys,

40    Wanton in fullness, seek to hide themselves
In drops of sorrow.—Sons, kinsmen, thanes,
And you whose places are the nearest, know
We will establish our estate upon
Our eldest, Malcolm, whom we name hereafter

45    The Prince of Cumberland;* which honour must
Not unaccompanied invest him only,
But signs of nobleness, like stars, shall shine
On all deservers.—From hence to Inverness,*
And bind us further to you.

**MACBETH**

50    The rest is labour which is not used for you.
I'll be myself the **harbinger** and make joyful
The hearing of my wife with your approach;
So humbly take my leave.

**DUNCAN**
My worthy Cawdor!

---

45    *Prince of Cumberland* At the time of Duncan's reign the throne of Scotland was
      not hereditary. If the King's successor was designated during the monarch's
      lifetime, he received the title of Prince of Cumberland as a sign of his future
      succession.

48    *Inverness* a Scottish town. Specifically the reference is to Macbeth's castle there.

are like children and servants to your throne and nation;
in doing all they can to safeguard you with love and honor,
they only do what they should. 30

**DUNCAN**
You are welcome here.
I have planted you, and will do all I can
to make sure that you grow well.—Noble Banquo,
you are no less deserving, and it must not be
thought that you have done less; so let me embrace you 35
and hold you to my heart.

**BANQUO**
If I grow there,
the harvest will belong to you.

**DUNCAN**
My countless joys
are unrestrained, and try to hide themselves 40
in teardrops.—Sons, kinsmen, thanes,
and those among you nearest to me: Learn
that we will leave the throne to
our oldest son, Malcolm, whom we shall call the Prince of 45
    Cumberland
from now on. He will not be the only one honored in such a way,
for gifts of nobility will shine like stars
on all who deserve them. (*to* MACBETH) Let's leave here for
    Inverness,
where you'll make me even more indebted to you.

**MACBETH**
Anything is really labor if it isn't used in your service. 50
I'll be the messenger myself, and make my wife
joyful to hear that you are coming;
I humbly leave you now.

**DUNCAN**
My worthy Cawdor.

**MACBETH** [*aside*]

55    The Prince of Cumberland! That is a step
      On which I must fall down, or else o'erleap,
      For in my way it lies. Stars, hide your fires;
      Let not light see my black and deep desires!
      The eye wink at the hand; yet let that be
60    Which the eye fears, when it is done, to see.

         *Exit.*

**DUNCAN**
      True, worthy Banquo; he is full so valiant,
      And in his commendations I am fed;
      It is a banquet to me. Let's after him,
      Whose care is gone before to bid us welcome.
65    It is a **peerless** kinsman.

         *Flourish. Exeunt.*

**MACBETH** (*aside*)

The Prince of Cumberland! That is a step                     55
I must either fall down from or else leap over,
for it lies in my way. Stars, hide your fires;
let not my black and deep desires be revealed by the light.
Let my eye not notice what my hand does—yet let my eye
see the deed it fears to see when it is done.                60

*He exits.*

**DUNCAN**

That's true, worthy Banquo. He is full of valor,
and I feel fed by the praises he receives;
it's like a banquet to me. Let's follow him,
since he's gone on ahead to make ready our welcome.
He is an unrivaled relative.                                 65

*Fanfare. They exit.*

# ACT I, SCENE V

*[Inverness. Macbeth's castle.] Enter* MACBETH'S *wife, alone, with a letter.*

**LADY MACBETH** [*Reads.*]

"They met me in the day of success; and I have learned by
the perfect'st report, they have more in them than mortal
knowledge. When I burned in desire to question them
further, they made themselves air, into which they
5     vanished. Whiles I stood rapt in the wonder of it, came
missives from the King, who all-hailed me 'Thane of
Cawdor'; by which title, before, these Weïrd Sisters saluted
me, and referred me to the coming on of time, with 'Hail,
King that shalt be!' This have I thought good to deliver
10     thee, my dearest partner of greatness, that thou mightst
not lose the dues of rejoicing, by being ignorant of what
greatness is promised thee. Lay it to thy heart, and farewell."
Glamis thou art, and Cawdor, and shalt be
What thou art promised. Yet do I fear thy nature;
15     It is too full o' th' milk of human kindness
To catch the nearest way. Thou wouldst be great,
Art not without ambition, but without
The illness* should attend it. What thou wouldst highly,
That wouldst thou holily; wouldst not play false,
20     And yet wouldst wrongly win. Thou'd'st have, great Glamis,
That which cries "Thus thou must do," if thou have it;
And that which rather thou dost fear to do
Than wishest should be undone. Hie thee hither,
That I may pour my spirits in thine ear;
25     And **chastise** with the valour of my tongue
All that **impedes** thee from the golden round,
Which fate and metaphysical aid doth seem
To have thee crown'd withal.

     *Enter* MESSENGER.

What is your tidings?

---

18    *illness* the evil quality—ruthlessness—which should go along with ambition

# ACT 1, SCENE 5

*Inverness. Macbeth's castle.* LADY MACBETH *enters, reading a letter.*

**LADY MACBETH**
*The Witches met me in the day of victory, and I have learned
from reliable sources they know more than mortals do. When I
burned with desire to question them more, they made themselves
like the air and vanished into it. While I stood there, entranced* 5
*with wonder about all this, a messenger came from the King
and hailed me as Thane of Cawdor. Those Weïrd Sisters had
    saluted me
by that same title; referring to the future, they also said, 'Hail, King
that will be!' I thought it good to tell you all this, my dearest
partner in future greatness; you mustn't miss the rejoicing you* 10
*deserve by being ignorant of the greatness promised to you.
Hold  it close to your heart, and farewell.*
You are the Thane of Glamis, and also of Cawdor; and you will be
what has been promised. But I'm worried about your character;
it is too full of the milk of human kindness 15
to take the quickest way. You want to be great;
you're not without ambition; but you lack
the necessary wickedness. The thing you want most to do,
you want to do in a holy way; you don't want to do wrong
even to win something you can only get wrongly. Great Glamis, 20
    you want something
which cries out to you, "You have to do this," or else you can't have it;
and you're more likely to fear doing a thing now
than to wish it were undone later. Hurry here quickly,
so I can pour my thoughts in your ear
and scold away with my bold tongue 25
everything that stands between you and the crown,
for fate and supernatural aid seem
to have given you that crown.

    A MESSENGER *enters.*

What is your news?

**MESSENGER**

30      The King comes here tonight.

**LADY MACBETH**

                                    Thou'rt mad to say it!
        Is not thy master with him, who, were 't so,
        Would have inform'd for preparation?

**MESSENGER**

        So please you, it is true. Our thane is coming.
35      One of my fellows had the speed of him,
        Who, almost dead for breath, had scarcely more
        Than would make up his message.

**LADY MACBETH**

                                    Give him tending;
        He brings great news.

        *Exit* MESSENGER.

40                              The raven* himself is hoarse
        That croaks the fatal entrance of Duncan
        Under my battlements. Come, you spirits
        That tend on mortal thoughts, unsex* me here,
        And fill me from the crown to the toe top-full
45      Of direst cruelty! Make thick my blood.
        Stop up th' access and passage to remorse,
        That no compunctious visitings of nature
        Shake my fell purpose, nor keep peace between
        Th' effect and it! Come to my woman's breasts,
50      And take my milk for gall, you murd'ring ministers,
        Wherever in your sightless substances
        You wait on nature's mischief! Come, thick night,
        And pall thee in the dunnest smoke of hell,
        That my keen knife see not the wound it makes,
55      Nor heaven peep through the blanket of the dark,
        To cry "Hold, hold!"

            *Enter* MACBETH.

---

40      *raven*  a bird of ill-omen and fateful powers

43      *unsex*  Lady Macbeth is asking to be free of mercy and gentleness, qualities
        traditionally associated with the female sex.

**MESSENGER**

The King is coming here tonight. 30

**LADY MACBETH**

You are mad to say so.
Isn't your master with him? And if this were so,
wouldn't he have sent word for us to prepare?

**MESSENGER**

May it please you, it is true. Our thane is coming.
One of my fellows outran him on his way; 35
almost dead for lack of breath, he had barely enough breath left
to deliver his message.

**LADY MACBETH**

Go and assist him.
He brings great news.

      *MESSENGER exits.*

The raven himself is hoarse 40
from croaking the news of Duncan's fatal entrance
under my battlements. Come, you spirits
that watch over deadly thoughts; take away my womanliness
and fill me to the brim, from head to toe,
with the most dreadful cruelty! Make my blood thick; 45
make my feelings numb and incapable of pity,
so that no natural pangs of remorse should come
and shake my deadly purpose, nor stand in the way
of the achievement of that purpose. Come to my woman's **breasts**
and replace my milk with gall, you spirits that urge to murder, 50
wherever your invisible forms
are aiding the destructive forces of nature! Come, thick night,
and enshroud yourself in the darkest smoke of hell,
so that my sharp knife can't see the wound it makes,
nor heaven peep through the blanket of the dark 55
to cry, "Stop, stop!"

      *MACBETH enters.*

Great Glamis! Worthy Cawdor!
Greater than both, by the all-hail hereafter!
Thy letters have transported me beyond
60   This ignorant present, and I feel now
The future in the instant.

**MACBETH**

                    My dearest love,
Duncan comes here tonight.

**LADY MACBETH**

                     And when goes hence?

**MACBETH**

65   Tomorrow, as he purposes.

**LADY MACBETH**

                    O, never
Shall sun that morrow see!
Your face, my thane, is as a book where men
May read strange matters. To beguile the time,
70   Look like the time. Bear welcome in your eye,
Your hand, your tongue. Look like th' innocent flower,
But be the serpent under 't. He that's coming
Must be provided for: and you shall put
This night's great business into my dispatch;
75   Which shall to all our nights and days to come
Give solely sovereign sway and masterdom.

**MACBETH**

We will speak further.

**LADY MACBETH**

                  Only look up clear.
To alter favour ever is to fear.
80   Leave all the rest to me.

      *Exeunt.*

Great Glamis, worthy Cawdor—
and greater than both by a promise of future kingship!
Your letter has carried me beyond
the ignorance of the present, and I can now sense     60
the future in this very moment.

**MACBETH**
My dearest love,
Duncan comes here tonight.

**LADY MACBETH**
And when will he leave?

**MACBETH**
He intends to leave tomorrow.     65

**LADY MACBETH**
Oh, the sun
will never look upon that tomorrow!
Your face, my thane, is like a book where men
can read strange things. To deceive people,
you must suit your looks to the occasion. Show welcome into     70
    your eye,
hand, and tongue. Look like the innocent flower,
but be the serpent under it. He who is coming
must be provided for; so you will put
me in charge of this night's great business,
which will bring royal power and mastery to us alone     75
for all the rest of our nights and days.

**MACBETH**
We will speak further.

**LADY MACBETH**
Just keep an innocent look about you;
to change your expression will be dangerous.
Leave all the rest to me.     80

     *They exit.*

# ACT I, SCENE VI

[*Before Macbeth's castle.*] *Hautboys and torches. Enter* DUNCAN, MALCOLM, DONALBAIN, BANQUO, LENNOX, MACDUFF, ROSS, ANGUS, *and* ATTENDANTS.

**DUNCAN**

This castle hath a pleasant seat; the air
Nimbly and sweetly recommends itself
Unto our gentle senses.

**BANQUO**

                  This guest of summer,
5    The temple-haunting martlet,* does approve,
By his loved mansionry, that the heaven's breath
Smells wooingly here. No jutty, frieze,
Buttress, nor coign of vantage, but this bird
Hath made his pendant bed and **procreant** cradle.
10  Where they most breed and haunt, I have observed,
The air is delicate.

    *Enter* LADY [MACBETH].

**DUNCAN**

See, see, our honoured hostess!
The love that follows us sometime is our trouble,
Which still we thank as love.* Herein I teach you
15  How you shall bid God 'ild us for your pains
And thank us for your trouble.

**LADY MACBETH**

                All our service
In every point twice done and then done double
Were poor and single business to contend
20  Against those honours deep and broad wherewith
Your Majesty loads our house. For those of old,
And the late dignities heaped up to them,
We rest your hermits.

---

5   *martlet*  the house martin, a small European bird of the swallow family

14  *love*  In this instance, Duncan is speaking of the love of a subject for his monarch, that is, loyalty, a sense of duty to one's feudal lord.

# ACT 1, SCENE 6

*Before Macbeth's castle. Oboes and torches.* DUNCAN,
MALCOLM, DONALBAIN, BANQUO, LENNOX, MACDUFF, ROSS,
ANGUS, *and* SERVANTS *enter.*

**DUNCAN**
> This castle is on a pleasant site. The air
> comes forth lightly and sweetly
> to soothe our senses.

**BANQUO**
> This summer visitor,
> the church-dwelling martin, proves                                    5
> that heaven's wind breathes delightfully here
> by making this his favorite home. I see no projection, decoration,
> buttress, or available corner where this bird
> hasn't made his hanging nest, his cradle for breeding his young.
> In places where these birds breed and visit most, I have
>        observed                                                       10
> that the air is delicate.

>        LADY MACBETH *enters.*

**DUNCAN**
> Look, look, our honored hostess!
> Though the love we receive is sometimes troublesome,
> we must still be grateful for it. In saying this, I teach you
> to ask God to reward us for all your inconvenience               15
> and thank us for troubling you.

**LADY MACBETH**
> All the service we can do for you—
> even if it were all done twice, then doubled again—
> must be a poor, slight offering when weighed
> against those deep, broad honors                                     20
> that Your Majesty loads upon our house. Because of past honors,
> and the recent ones heaped upon them,
> we're obliged to pray for you.

**DUNCAN**

                               Where's the Thane of Cawdor?
25 We coursed him at the heels and had a purpose
To be his purveyor; but he rides well,
And his great love, sharp as his spur, hath holp him
To his home before us. Fair and noble hostess,
We are your guest tonight.

**LADY MACBETH**

30                                  Your servants ever
Have theirs, themselves, and what is theirs, in compt,
To make their audit at your Highness's pleasure,
Still to return your own.

**DUNCAN**

                             Give me your hand.
35 Conduct me to mine host: we love him highly,
And shall continue our graces towards him.
By your leave, hostess.

      *Exeunt.*

**DUNCAN**

    Where is the Thane of Cawdor?
    We pursued him at his heels and had intended         25
    to arrive before him. But he rides well,
    and his great love for you, as sharp as his spur, has helped him
    to reach home ahead of us. Fair and noble hostess,
    we are your guest tonight.

**LADY MACBETH**

    As your servants, we always         30
    keep our people, ourselves, and all that is ours ready to be
        accounted for,
    so that you can inspect them whenever you wish,
    and always receive what's yours.

**DUNCAN**

    Give me your hand. (*taking her hand*)
    Lead me to my host. We love him highly,         35
    and will continue to grant favors to him.
    With your permission, hostess.

        *They exit.*

# ACT I, SCENE VII

*[Macbeth's castle.] Hautboys and torches. Enter a* SEWER
*and divers* SERVANTS *with dishes and service over the
stage. Then enter* MACBETH.

**MACBETH**

If it were done when 'tis done, then 'twere well
It were done quickly. If the assassination
Could trammel up the consequence, and catch
With his surcease, success; that but this blow
Might be the be-all and the end-all—here,
But here, upon this bank and shoal of time,
We'd jump the life to come. But in these cases
We still have judgment here; that we but teach
Bloody instructions, which, being taught, return
To plague th' inventor: this even-handed justice
Commends th' ingredients of our poison'd chalice
To our own lips. He's here in double trust:
First, as I am his kinsman and his subject,
Strong both against the deed; then, as his host,
Who should against his murderer shut the door,
Not bear the knife myself. Besides, this Duncan
Hath borne his faculties so meek, hath been
So clear in his great office, that his virtues
Will plead like angels, trumpet-tongued against
The deep damnation of his taking-off;
And pity, like a naked newborn babe,
Striding the blast, or heaven's cherubin horsed
Upon the sightless couriers of the air,
Shall blow the horrid deed in every eye,
That tears shal¹ drown the wind. I have no spur
To prick the sides of my intent, but only
Vaulting ambition, which o'erleaps itself
And falls on the other—

    *Enter* LADY MACBETH.

How now, what news?

# ACT 1, SCENE 7

*A room in Macbeth's castle. Oboes and torches. A chief* BUTLER
*and several* SERVANTS *enter with dishes and utensils and pass
across the stage. Then* MACBETH *enters.*

**MACBETH**
If it's over with once it's been done, then it would be best
to do it quickly. If the murder
could gather up the consequences in a net, achieving
success through his death, and if this deed
could prove sufficient all by itself—then here,                    5
right here, upon time's riverbank,
I'd risk my eternal life. But in a case like this,
I still might be judged in this life; I might also teach others
to do bloody deeds—and once those lessons are taught,
they might be turned against me. This impartial justice           10
offers the poisonous ingredients of my cup to my own lips.
    He has two reasons to trust me while he's here:
First, I am his relative and his subject—
and as both, I have strong reasons not to do the deed. Second, I
    am his host,
who should shut the door to keep out his murderer,               15
not hold the knife myself. Besides, this Duncan
has wielded power so mildly, and his reign
has been so blameless, that his virtues
will plead like trumpet-voiced angels to protest
the damnable crime of his murder;                                20
and pity will be like a naked, newborn infant
straddling the wind, or like heaven's cherubim riding
the invisible horses of the air—
for pity will blow the horrid deed into every eye
so that tears will drown the wind. I have nothing               25
to spur me on toward my intended deed
except ambition, which leaps over itself
and falls on the other side—

    LADY MACBETH *enters.*

Well, then—what is your news?

**LADY MACBETH**

30      He has almost supped. Why have you left the chamber?

**MACBETH**

Hath he asked for me?

**LADY MACBETH**

Know you not he has?

**MACBETH**

We will proceed no further in this business.
He hath honour'd me of late; and I have bought
35      Golden opinions from all sorts of people,
Which would be worn now in their newest gloss,
Not cast aside so soon.

**LADY MACBETH**

Was the hope drunk
Wherein you dressed yourself? Hath it slept since?
40      And wakes it now, to look so green and pale
At what it did so freely? From this time
Such I account thy love. Art thou afeard
To be the same in thine own act and valor
As thou art in desire? Wouldst thou have that
45      Which thou esteem'st the ornament of life,
And live a coward in thine own esteem,
Letting "I dare not" wait upon "I would,"
Like the poor cat i' th' adage?*

**MACBETH**

Prithee, peace!
50      I dare do all that may become a man;
Who dares do more is none.

**LADY MACBETH**

What beast was 't then,
That made you break this enterprise to me?
When you durst do it, then you were a man;
55      And to be more than what you were, you would
Be so much more the man. Nor time nor place
Did then adhere, and yet you would make both.

---

48      *poor cat i' th' adage*  a familiar saying about a cat that wanted fish, but was
unwilling to wet her feet to catch them

**LADY MACBETH**
He has almost eaten. Why did you leave the chamber?          30

**MACBETH**
Has he asked for me?

**LADY MACBETH**
Don't you know that he has?

**MACBETH**
We will go no further in this business.
He has honored me lately, and I have gained
the golden respect of all sorts of people—          35
and this respect should be worn while it is shiny and new,
not cast aside so soon.

**LADY MACBETH**
Was it only a drunken hope
that you wore before? Has it been sleeping since?
Is it waking up now, looking sickly and pale          40
at what it meant to do so freely? From now on,
I'll value your love as equally fickle. Are you afraid
to show the boldness and action needed
to become what you want to be? Would you be content to have
the crown you value so highly,          45
and yet live, in your own opinion, a coward's life?
Are you willing to let the words "I don't dare" come after the
    words "I want to,"
like the poor cat in the proverb?

**MACBETH**
I implore you, be quiet.
I dare do all that's worthy of a man.          50
Whoever dares to do more is not a man.

**LADY MACBETH**
So what kind of beast was it
that first made you tell me about this scheme?
When you dared to do it, you were a man;
and to be more than what you were then          55
would make you even more of a man. Neither the time nor the
    place
were then ready, and yet you were willing to make them both
    ready.

They have made themselves, and that their fitness now
Does unmake you. I have given suck, and know
How tender 'tis to love the babe that milks me.
I would, while it was smiling in my face,
Have pluck'd my nipple from his boneless gums,
And dashed the brains out, had I so sworn as you
Have done to this.

**MACBETH**

If we should fail?

**LADY MACBETH**

We fail?
But screw your courage to the sticking-place,*
And we'll not fail. When Duncan is asleep—
Whereto the rather shall his day's hard journey
Soundly invite him—his two chamberlains
Will I with wine and wassail so convince
That memory, the warder of the brain,
Shall be a fume, and the receipt of reason
A limbeck* only: when in swinish sleep
Their drenched natures lie as in a death,
What cannot you and I perform upon
Th' unguarded Duncan? What not put upon
His spongy officers, who shall bear the guilt
Of our great quell?

**MACBETH**

Bring forth men-children only;
For thy undaunted mettle should compose
Nothing but males. Will it not be received,
When we have marked with blood those sleepy two
Of his own chamber and used their very daggers,
That they have done 't?

**LADY MACBETH**

Who dares receive it other,
As we shall make our griefs and clamour roar

---

67  *screw your courage to the sticking-place*  This usage may refer to the tightening of
the cord on a crossbow to the "sticking-place" (i.e., making it as taut as possible
and ready to be shot).

74  *limbeck*  "alembic," a word derived from the Moorish alchemists of Spain. It was
an instrument used in distillation.

Now they have made themselves ready, and their readiness
makes you unsure of yourself. I have nursed a child, and I know
how sweet it is to love the baby that sucks milk from me.          60
And yet, while he was smiling in my face,
I would have plucked my nipple from his boneless gums
and dashed his brains out, if I had sworn
to do this as you have sworn.

**MACBETH**
If we should fail—                                                  65

**LADY MACBETH**
We fail?
Just fasten your courage to the notch,
and we'll not fail. When Duncan is asleep—
and after his day's hard journey,
he'll soon sleep soundly—I'll overpower                             70
his two chamber servants with wine and revelry
until memory, the guard of the brain,
is smoky, and the container that catches reason
is nothing but an alembic. When they are sleeping like pigs,
lying there drenched in alcohol as if they were dead,               75
what won't you and I be able to do
to the unguarded Duncan? What won't be blamed upon
his drunken officers, who will bear the guilt
of our great murder?

**MACBETH**
Give birth only to but men-children,                                80
for your bold spirit should create
nothing but males. When we have smeared
his two sleepy chamber guards with his blood
and used their own daggers, won't everyone believe
that they have done it?                                             85

**LADY MACBETH**
Who'll dare believe anything else,
since we shall roar and howl with grief

Upon his death?

**MACBETH**

                    I am settled and bend up
90     Each corporal agent to this terrible feat.
Away, and mock the time with fairest show:
False face must hide what the false heart doth know.

     *Exeunt.*

upon his death?

**MACBETH**

    I am determined, and strain

    every muscle to ready myself for this terrible feat.         90

    Let's go, and trick the world with our pleasant looks.

    Our false faces must hide what we know in our false hearts.

      *They exit.*

# Act I Review

## Discussion Questions

1. Why do you think Shakespeare used a scene with three witches to begin this play? Think about how this beginning might prepare the audience for what is to come.

2. Contrast the way Banquo and Macbeth react to the Witches.

3. Describe what kind of man King Duncan is. Do you think he is a good leader? Explain.

4. In your opinion, what is Lady Macbeth's attitude toward her husband? Give examples from the text to support your answer.

5. Reread King Duncan's speech in Act I, Scene iv, lines 13–24, and discuss why you think Shakespeare had Duncan say this just before Macbeth enters. Do you agree with King Duncan that you cannot tell what people are really like just by looking at them?

6. List the steps of Lady Macbeth's plan to kill King Duncan and blame it on someone else. Next to each step, write possible things that could go wrong.

7. What does Macbeth credit with giving him the courage to do the deed?

## Literary Elements

1. Images of blood and darkness run through the entire play of Macbeth. Find as many examples of this **imagery** as possible in Act I.

2. A **simile** makes a comparison of two unlike things using *like* or *as*. Find one or two similes in Act I and explain how each helps to convey the feeling of the play.

3. Shakespeare allows his characters to reveal their innermost thoughts and feelings to the audience through speeches called **soliloquies**. What ideas about murdering Duncan does Macbeth express in his soliloquy in Scene vii?

4. A **euphemism** is a phrase that softens reality; for example, people often use the phrase "passed away" instead of "died." Note all the euphemisms Macbeth uses in his soliloquy in Scene vii in place of the words "killing Duncan." Substitute "killing Duncan" to see what difference it makes, if any.

# Writing Prompts

1. Macbeth might have stopped thinking about killing Duncan if his wife hadn't urged him on. Write about a time that a person convinced you to do something you weren't sure about. Tell what that person did to persuade you. Then explain if that person's advice hurt or helped you.

2. What if, like Macbeth, you got the chance to discover your future? Divide a piece of paper into two columns. Then list the advantages and disadvantages of knowing your future. Afterward decide if you would take the risk of learning what your future looks like. Explain your decision in writing.

3. Write a news report about the recent battles. Refer to the information that was presented to King Duncan by the Captain and Ross.

4. Act I, Scene v begins with Lady Macbeth reading the ending of a letter from her husband, Macbeth. Keeping true to all of the information you have from the play so far, write the beginning of the letter. Remember to tell Lady Macbeth about the recent battle.

# Macbeth
## ACT II

Pat Hingle and Jessica Tandy as Macbeth and Lady Macbeth

"Will all great Neptune's ocean wash
this blood clean from my hand?"

# Before You Read

1. Think of a time when you relied on someone who was untrustworthy. How might you feel if a trusted friend turned against you?

2. Who seems more determined to kill Duncan—Macbeth or Lady Macbeth?

3. As you read, consider who, if anyone, seems to suspect Macbeth.

# Literary Elements

1. **Comic relief** allows a playwright to include elements of humor in plays that are otherwise serious. These humorous interludes give the audience a break from the dramatic tension of the rest of the story.

2. A **double entendre** is a statement that has two different meanings, one of which may be sexual. In Act I, Scene v, Lady Macbeth asks the spirits to "unsex" her. This can mean both "turn her into a man" and "free her of mercy and gentleness," qualities associated with women.

3. **Conflict** is what creates tension and drama in a piece of writing. **External conflict** refers to a struggle between an individual and an outside force, such as nature or another individual. **Internal conflict** refers to a mental struggle within the individual. There is external conflict between Macbeth and Lady Macbeth, who is pushing him harder to be more ruthless. And Macbeth suffers internal conflict because he badly wants to be King but knows that murdering Duncan is wrong.

# Words to Know

The following vocabulary words appear in Act II in the original text of Shakespeare's play. However, they are words that are still commonly used. Read the definitions here and pay attention to the words as you read the play (they will be in boldfaced type).

| | |
|---|---|
| **augment** | enlarge; increase |
| **clamored** [clamour'd] | made a lot of noise |
| **consort** | associate or partner with |
| **entreat** | request; implore |
| **largess** | generosity; charity |
| **malice** | hatred; hostility |
| **multitudinous** | plentiful; ample |
| **palpable** | touchable; tangible |
| **pretense** | excuse; evasion |
| **repose** | rest; relaxation |
| **suborned** | bribed; urged secretly to do something illegal |
| **temperate** [temp'rate] | moderate; calm |

# Act Summary

King Duncan and his followers eat and drink until the King is ready for bed. Lady Macbeth drugs the King's guards, putting them in a deep sleep. Then, while Duncan sleeps, Macbeth creeps into his room and murders him with the sleeping guards' daggers.

Macbeth is immediately horrified by his own deed and hears a voice telling him that he will never sleep again. Deeply shaken, he leaves the room, forgetting something very important—to make it appear that the guards committed the murder. Lady Macbeth takes the daggers back to Duncan's room and smears the sleeping guards with the King's blood.

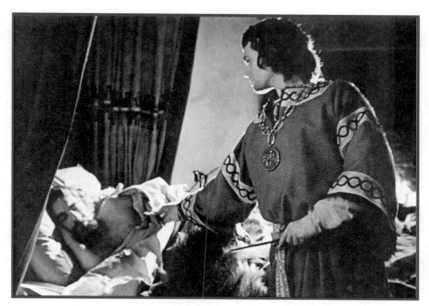
Macbeth preparing to kill Duncan, Polanski film, 1971

Morning dawns. Macduff, the Thane of Fife, goes to Duncan's chamber to wake the King. Horrified at discovering the murder, he alerts the castle.

Macbeth returns to the King's room and kills the guards. He tells his guests that he did it out of rage over their obvious guilt.

Fearing for their lives, the King's sons, Malcolm and Donalbain, flee the country. This makes them look guilty of having plotted their father's murder.

# ACT II, SCENE I

[*Inverness. Court of Macbeth's castle.*] *Enter* BANQUO
*and* FLEANCE, *with a torch before him.*

**BANQUO**
How goes the night, boy?

**FLEANCE**
The moon is down; I have not heard the clock.

**BANQUO**
And she goes down at twelve.

**FLEANCE**
I take 't, 'tis later, sir.

**BANQUO**
5   Hold, take my sword. There's husbandry in heaven;
Their candles are all out. Take thee that too.
A heavy summons lies like lead upon me,
And yet I would not sleep. Merciful powers,
Restrain in me the cursed thoughts that nature
10  Gives way to in repose!

*Enter* MACBETH *and a* SERVANT *with a torch.*

Give me my sword.
Who's there?

**MACBETH**
A friend.

**BANQUO**
What, sir, not yet at rest? The King's a-bed:
15  He hath been in unusual pleasure, and
Sent forth great **largess** to your offices.
This diamond he greets your wife withal,
By the name of most kind hostess, and shut up
In measureless content.

# ACT 2, SCENE 1

    *Court of Macbeth's castle. BANQUO and FLEANCE enter;*
    FLEANCE *carries a torch.*

**BANQUO**

What time of night is it, boy?

**FLEANCE**

The moon is down. I haven't heard the clock strike.

**BANQUO**

The moon goes down at midnight.

**FLEANCE**

I believe it is later, sir.

**BANQUO**

Wait, take my sword. There's thrift in heaven;      5
its candles are all out. Take that, too.
An urgent need to sleep lies upon me like lead,
and yet I do not wish to sleep. Merciful God,
keep away from me those cursed thoughts
that come to me whenever I rest!      10

     MACBETH *and a* SERVANT *enter, the* SERVANT *with a torch.*

Give me my sword.
Who's there?

**MACBETH**

A friend.

**BANQUO**

What's this, sir! Aren't you asleep yet? The King's in bed.
He has been enjoying himself more than usual,      15
and gave enormous tips to your servants.
He sent this diamond to your wife,
greeting her by the name of most kind hostess. Now his day has
    ended
in perfect happiness.

    *He gives* MACBETH *a diamond.*

**MACBETH**

20                              Being unprepared,
Our will became the servant to defect,
Which else should free have wrought.

**BANQUO**

All's well.
I dreamt last night of the three Weïrd Sisters:
25    To you they have show'd some truth.

**MACBETH**

                                    I think not of them.
Yet, when we can **entreat** an hour to serve,
We would spend it in some words upon that business,
If you would grant the time.

**BANQUO**

30                              At your kind'st leisure.

**MACBETH**

If you shall cleave to my consent, when 'tis,
It shall make honour for you.

**BANQUO**

                        So I lose none
In seeking to **augment** it, but still keep
35    My bosom franchised and allegiance clear,
I shall be counseled.

**MACBETH**

Good **repose** the while!

**BANQUO**

                    Thanks, sir. The like to you!

*Exit* BANQUO [*with* FLEANCE].

**MACBETH**

Go bid thy mistress, when my drink is ready,
40    She strike upon the bell. Get thee to bed.

*Exit* [SERVANT].

Is this a dagger which I see before me,
The handle toward my hand? Come, let me clutch thee!
I have thee not, and yet I see thee still.

**MACBETH**

Since we were unprepared for his visit,                   20
our desire to serve him was greater than our ability to do so;
otherwise, we would have been more generous.

**BANQUO**

It's all right.
I dreamed last night of the three Witches.
To you, they have shown some truth.                      25

**MACBETH**

I don't think about them.
And yet, whenever we get an hour to ourselves,
we should spend it talking some about that business—
if you'll allow the time.

**BANQUO**

Whenever you wish.                                        30

**MACBETH**

If you'll ally yourself with me at the proper moment,
you'll gain honors by it.

**BANQUO**

As long as I lose no honor
in seeking to add to what I already have—always keeping
my heart free from evil and my loyalties spotless—       35
I'll hear what you have to say.

**MACBETH**

Meanwhile, sleep well.

**BANQUO**

Thanks, sir. The same to you.

> BANQUO *and* FLEANCE *exit.*

**MACBETH** (*to a* SERVANT)

Go tell your mistress to ring the bell
when my drink is ready. Go on to bed.                    40

> SERVANT *exits.*

Is this a dagger that I see before me,
its handle pointed toward my hand? Come here—let me grab
    you.
I can't hold you, and yet I still see you.

Art thou not, fatal vision, sensible
45     To feeling as to sight? Or art thou but
A dagger of the mind, a false creation,
Proceeding from the heat-oppressed brain?
I see thee yet, in form as **palpable**
As this which now I draw.
50     Thou marshal'st me the way that I was going;
And such an instrument I was to use.
Mine eyes are made the fools o' th' other senses,
Or else worth all the rest. I see thee still;
And on thy blade and dudgeon gouts of blood,
55     Which was not so before. There's no such thing.
It is the bloody business which informs
Thus to mine eyes. Now o'er the one half-world
Nature seems dead, and wicked dreams abuse
The curtained sleep. Witchcraft celebrates
60     Pale Hecate's* off'rings, and withered murder,
Alarum'd by his sentinel, the wolf,
Whose howl's his watch, thus with his stealthy pace.
With Tarquin's* ravishing strides, towards his design
Moves like a ghost. Thou sure and firm-set earth,
65     Hear not my steps, which way they walk, for fear
Thy very stones prate of my whereabout,
And take the present horror from the time,
Which now suits with it. Whiles I threat, he lives.
Words to the heat of deeds too cold breath gives.

       *A bell rings.*

70     I go, and it is done. The bell invites me.
Hear it not, Duncan; for it is a knell
That summons thee to heaven or to hell.

       *Exit.*

---

60   *Hecate* the classical goddess of magic and witchcraft

63   *Tarquin* Sextus Tarquinius, noted for his tyranny and arrogance. When the
Roman people (6th century B.C.) saw the virtuous Lucrece stab herself after
being ravished by Tarquin, they rose and expelled the Tarquin family from Rome.

Fearful vision, can't you be felt by my touch
as well as seen? Or are you nothing but                          45
a dagger of my imagination, a false creation
that comes from my feverish brain?
I still see you, looking just as solid
as this dagger I now draw.

     *He draws his dagger.*

You lead me the way I was going,                                 50
and just such a weapon I am supposed to use.
Either my eyes are more foolish than my other senses,
or they are worth all the rest together. I still see you—
and on your blade and handle, I see large drops of blood
that weren't there before. There's no such thing as this dagger.  55
My bloody business causes it to take shape
before my eyes in this way. Now over this half of the world,
nature seems dead, and wicked dreams deceive
those who are hidden in sleep. Witchcraft celebrates
the ceremonies of pale Hecate; and withered murder            60
is awakened by his guard, the wolf,
whose howl is his cry of warning; and so, at a stealthy pace,
murder moves with Tarquin's lustful footsteps toward his goal
like a ghost. You solid and firmly set earth,
don't hear my steps or which way they walk, for I fear         65
that even your stones might tell where I am,
breaking the horrible silence
that suits this moment well. While I threaten to act, he lives.
Words cool hot deeds too much with their cold breath.

     *A bell rings.*

I go, and the murder will be done. The bell calls for me to do it.  70
Do not hear it, Duncan, for this ringing
summons you to heaven or to hell.

     *Exit.*

# ACT II, SCENE II

[*Macbeth's castle.*] *Enter* LADY [MACBETH].

**LADY MACBETH**
That which hath made them drunk hath made me bold;
What hath quench'd them hath given me fire. Hark! Peace!
It was the owl that shriek'd, the fatal bellman,
Which gives the stern'st good-night.* He is about it.
5   The doors are open, and the surfeited grooms
Do mock their charge with snores: I have drugged
    their possets,
That death and nature do contend about them,
Whether they live or die.

**MACBETH** [*within*]
10                   Who's there? What, ho?

**LADY MACBETH**
Alack, I am afraid they have awaked,
And 'tis not done. Th' attempt and not the deed
Confounds us. Hark! I laid their daggers ready;
He could not miss 'em. Had he not resembled
15   My father as he slept, I had done 't.

       *Enter* MACBETH.

                       My husband?

**MACBETH**
I have done the deed. Didst thou not hear a noise?

**LADY MACBETH**
I heard the owl scream and the crickets cry.
Did not you speak?

**MACBETH**
20           When?

**LADY MACBETH**
           Now.

**MACBETH**
                 As I descended?

---

4   *stern'st good-night* According to superstition, the owl's hoot foretells death. In this
image the owl is seen as a bellman or town crier visiting the condemned prisoner
on the night before his execution.

# ACT 2, SCENE 2

*Court of Macbeth's castle.* LADY MACBETH *enters.*

**LADY MACBETH**
The wine that has made them drunk has made me bold;
it has put them to sleep, but has inflamed my courage. Listen!
　　Hush!
It was the owl that shrieked—the fatal crier,
who calls out a stern good night. My husband is doing it.
The doors are open, and the drunken guards　　　　　　5
mock their duties with snores. I have drugged their nighttime
　　drink so that death and life argue with one another
as to whether the men are alive or dead.

**MACBETH** (*offstage*)
Who's there? What's this?　　　　　　　　　　　　　10

**LADY MACBETH**
Oh, no! I'm afraid they have awakened,
and it's not been done. We are ruined by the attempt,
not by the deed. Listen! I laid out their daggers so they'd be ready;
Macbeth couldn't miss them. If the king hadn't looked
like my father while he slept, I would have done it myself.　　15

　　　　　MACBETH *enters with bloody daggers.*

My husband?

**MACBETH**
I have done the deed. Didn't you hear a noise?

**LADY MACBETH**
I heard the owl scream and the crickets cry.
Didn't you speak?

**MACBETH**
When?　　　　　　　　　　　　　　　　　　　20

**LADY MACBETH**
Just now.

**MACBETH**
While I was coming down?

**LADY MACBETH**
Ay.

**MACBETH**
Hark!
25 Who lies i' the second chamber?

**LADY MACBETH**
Donalbain.

**MACBETH**
This is a sorry sight.

**LADY MACBETH**
A foolish thought, to say a sorry sight.

**MACBETH**
There's one did laugh in 's sleep, and one cried "Murder!"
30 That they did wake each other. I stood and heard them.
But they did say their prayers, and addressed them
Again to sleep.

**LADY MACBETH**
There are two lodged together.

**MACBETH**
One cried "God bless us!" and "Amen" the other,
35 As they had seen me with these hangman's hands,
List'ning their fear, I could not say "Amen,"
When they did say "God bless us!"

**LADY MACBETH**
                                                    Consider it not so deeply.

**MACBETH**
But wherefore could not I pronounce "Amen"?
40 I had most need of blessing, and "Amen"
Stuck in my throat.

**LADY MACBETH**
                          These deeds must not be thought
After these ways; so, it will make us mad.

**MACBETH**
Methought I heard a voice cry "Sleep no more!
45 Macbeth does murder sleep"— the innocent sleep,
Sleep that knits up the ravell'd sleave of care,

**LADY MACBETH**
Yes.

**MACBETH**
Listen!
Who's sleeping in the second room?                                      25

**LADY MACBETH**
Donalbain.

**MACBETH** *(looking at his bloody hands)*
This is a miserable sight.

**LADY MACBETH**
How foolish—to call it a miserable sight.

**MACBETH**
One of them laughed in his sleep, and the other cried, "Murder!"
And so they woke each other up. I stood and listened to them.      30
But they said their prayers, and then they settled down
to go back to sleep.

**LADY MACBETH**
Two of them are in that room together.

**MACBETH**
One cried, "God bless us!" And the other cried, "Amen!"
It was as if they had seen me with these executioner's hands,     35
listening in on their fear. I could not say "Amen"
when they said "God bless us."

**LADY MACBETH**
Don't think about it too deeply.

**MACBETH**
But why couldn't I say the word "Amen"?
I was in great need of a blessing, but "Amen"                         40
stuck in my throat.

**LADY MACBETH**
Such deeds must not be thought about
in such a way; otherwise, they will drive us mad.

**MACBETH**
I thought I heard a voice cry, "Sleep no more!
Macbeth murders sleep"—the innocent sleep,                        45
sleep that straightens out the tangled skein of worry;

The death of each day's life, sore labour's bath,
Balm of hurt minds, great nature's second course,
Chief nourisher in life's feast—

**LADY MACBETH**

50                                              What do you mean?

**MACBETH**

Still it cried "Sleep no more!" to all the house:
"Glamis hath murder'd sleep, and therefore Cawdor
Shall sleep no more. Macbeth shall sleep no more."

**LADY MACBETH**

Who was it that thus cried? Why, worthy thane,
55      You do unbend your noble strength, to think
So brainsickly of things. Go get some water,
And wash this filthy witness from your hand.
Why did you bring these daggers from the place?
They must lie there. Go carry them, and smear
60      The sleepy grooms with blood.

**MACBETH**

                                                    I'll go no more:
I am afraid to think what I have done;
Look on 't again I dare not.

**LADY MACBETH**

                                          Infirm of purpose!
65      Give me the daggers. The sleeping and the dead
Are but as pictures. 'Tis the eye of childhood
That fears a painted devil. If he do bleed,
I'll gild the faces of the grooms withal,
For it must seem their guilt.

            *Exit. Knock within.*

**MACBETH**

70                                      Whence is that knocking?
How is 't with me, when every noise appalls me?
What hands are here? Ha! They pluck out mine eyes.
Will all great Neptune's* ocean wash this blood

---

73    *Neptune*  the Roman god of the sea

the death of each day's life; a soothing bath after hard labor;
an ointment for hurt minds; the second course of great nature's
    meal;
the most nutritious part of life's feast.

**LADY MACBETH**

What do you mean?                                                          50

**MACBETH**

It kept crying, "Sleep no more!" to everyone in the house.
"The Thane of Glamis has murdered sleep—and so the Thane
    of Cawdor
will sleep no more. Macbeth will sleep no more."

**LADY MACBETH**

Who was it that cried in such a way? Why, worthy Thane,
you slacken your noble strength in thinking                                 55
so squeamishly about things. Go, get some water,
and wash this filthy evidence off your hand.
Why did you bring these daggers from the place?
They must stay there. Go—carry them back, and smear
the sleeping guards with blood.                                            60

**MACBETH**

I won't go anymore.
I'm afraid to even think about what I've done;
I don't dare look at it again.

**LADY MACBETH**

How indecisive you are!
Give me the daggers. The sleeping and the dead                             65
are like pictures, nothing more. Only the eye of a child
fears a painted devil. If Duncan is bleeding,
I'll paint the faces of the servants with his blood,
for they must seem guilty of the murder.

> LADY MACBETH *exits. Knocking offstage.*

**MACBETH**

Where is that knocking coming from?                                        70
What's wrong with me, that every noise terrifies me?
(looking at his hands) Whose hands are these? Ha! They'll pluck
    out my eyes.
Could all of great Neptune's ocean wash my hand

Clean from my hand? No, this my hand will rather
75    The **multitudinous** seas in incarnadine,
Making the green one red.

          *Enter* LADY [MACBETH].

**LADY MACBETH**
My hands are of your colour; but I shame
To wear a heart so white. [*knocking*] I hear a knocking
At the south entry. Retire we to our chamber;
80    A little water clears us of this deed:
How easy is it, then! Your constancy
Hath left you unattended. [*knocking*] Hark!
          More knocking.
Get on your nightgown, lest occasion call us,
85    And show us to be watchers. Be not lost
So poorly in your thoughts.

**MACBETH**
To know my deed, 'twere best not know myself. [*knocking*]
Wake Duncan with thy knocking! I would thou couldst!

          *Exeunt.*

clean of this blood? No; instead, my hand
would drench the enormous seas a crimson color,                    75
making their green waters wholly red.

    LADY MACBETH *reenters.*

**LADY MACBETH**

My hands are red like yours, but I'd be ashamed
to wear a heart so white. (*knocking offstage*) I hear a knocking
at the south entry. Let's go to our bedroom.
A little water will wash all signs of this deed off us:            80
how easy it will all be, then! Your self-assurance
has deserted you. (*knocking within*) Listen, more knocking.
Put on your dressing gown, or someone may call on us
and realize that we've been awake. Don't be so weak               85
and lost in thought.

**MACBETH**

To know what I have done—it would be better to lose
consciousness altogether. (*knocking offstage*)
Wake up Duncan with your knocking! I wish you could!

    *They exit.*

# ACT II, SCENE III

[*Macbeth's castle.*] *Enter a* PORTER. *Knocking within.*

**PORTER**

Here's a knocking indeed! If a man were porter of hell
gate, he should have old turning the key. [*knocking*]
Knock, knock, knock! Who's there, i' th' name of
Beelzebub?* Here's a farmer, that hanged himself on the
5   expectation of plenty.* Come in time! Have napkins enow
about you; here you'll sweat for 't. [*knocking*] Knock,
knock! Who's there, in th' other devil's name. Faith, here's
an equivocator* that could swear in both the scales
against either scale; who committed treason enough for
10  God's sake, yet could not equivocate to heaven. O, come
in, equivocator. [*knocking*] Knock, knock, knock! Who's
there? Faith, here's an English tailor come hither for
stealing out of a French hose:* come in, tailor. Here you
may roast your goose.* [*knocking*] Knock, knock; never at
15  quiet! What are you? But this place is too cold for hell. I'll
devil-porter it no further. I had thought to have let in
some of all professions that go the primrose way to th'
everlasting bonfire. [*knocking*] Anon, anon! [*Opens an
entrance.*] I pray you, remember the porter.

*Enter* MACDUFF *and* LENNOX.

**MACDUFF**

20  Was it so late, friend, ere you went to bed,
That you do lie so late?

---

4   *Beelzebub* In Matthew 12:24, Beelzebub is spoken of as "the prince of the devils."

5   *expectation of plenty* Probably this means that the farmer expected to sell hoarded grain at high prices, but abundant crops caused the supply to exceed the demand and he lost his investment.

8   *equivocator* One who uses double-meanings to confuse his listeners. Shakespeare may have had in mind the Jesuit, Henry Garnet, Superior of the Society of Jesus in England. He stood trial on March 28, 1606, for participating in the Gunpowder Plot. He later confessed to equivocating at the trial—to perjury, his enemies said—and was hanged.

# ACT 2, SCENE 3

*Court of Macbeth's castle. Knocking offstage. A PORTER enters.*

**PORTER**

Here's a knocking, indeed! If a man were the porter of the gate of
hell, he'd have to turn the key a whole lot. *(knocking offstage)*
Knock, knock, knock! Who's there, in the name of Beelzebub?
Here's a farmer who hanged himself because he'd hoped for
higher prices. Welcome to you! Bring plenty of handkerchiefs      5
to keep yourself dry; you'll do some sweating here. *(knocking
offstage)* Knock, knock! Who's there, in some other devil's name?
Why here's an equivocator who could swear different things in
each of the scales of justice; he committed treason in the name of
God, but couldn't equivocate his way to heaven. Oh, come in,      10
equivocator. *(knocking offstage)* Knock, knock, knock! Who's there?
Why, here's an English tailor who's come here because he stole
fabric out of tight-fitting pants. Come in, tailor. Here you can heat
up your pressing iron. *(knocking offstage)* Knock, knock! Never any
quiet. Who are you? But this place is too cold for hell. I'll stop      15
playing the devil-porter. I'd planned to let in folks from all the
professions that go the wide and easy path to eternal damnation.
*(knocking offstage)* Right away! *(Opens a door.)* I ask you to
remember to tip the porter.

MACDUFF *and* LENNOX *enter.*

**MACDUFF**

Friend, is it because you went to bed so late      20
that you arise so late?

---

13    *French hose* Certain types of French trousers fitted so tightly that even a
      dishonest tailor had trouble stealing surplus material while making them.

14    *goose* tailor's pressing iron

**PORTER**

Faith, sir, we were carousing till the second cock:* and drink, sir, is a great provoker of three things.

**MACDUFF**

What three things does drink especially provoke?

**PORTER**

25    Marry, sir, nose-painting, sleep, and urine. Lechery, sir, it provokes, and unprovokes; it provokes the desire, but it takes away the performance: therefore, much drink may be said to be an equivocator with lechery. It makes him, and it mars him; it sets him on, and it takes him off; it
30    persuades him and disheartens him; makes him stand to and not stand to; in conclusion, equivocates him in a sleep, and giving him the lie, leaves him.

**MACDUFF**

I believe drink gave thee the lie last night.

**PORTER**

That it did, sir, i' th' very throat on me; but I requited
35    him for his lie; and, I think, being too strong for him, though he took up my legs sometime, yet I made a shift to cast him.

**MACDUFF**

Is thy master stirring?

*Enter* MACBETH.

Our knocking has awaked him; here he comes.

[PORTER *exits.*]

**LENNOX**

40    Good morrow, noble sir.

**MACBETH**

Good morrow, both.

**MACDUFF**

Is the King stirring, worthy Thane?

**MACBETH**

Not yet.

---

22    *second cock* second cockcrow or about 3 a.m.

**PORTER**

Why, sir, we were partying till 3 o'clock a.m., and drink, sir, is a great cause of three things.

**MACDUFF**

What three things does drink cause most?

**PORTER**

Goodness sir, red noses, sleep, and urine. Lechery, sir, it           25
causes and uncauses. It causes the desire, but it makes it
difficult to perform. And so, heavy drinking might be called
an equivocator as far as lechery is concerned. It helps him,
and it hurts him; it turns him on, and it turns him off; it
encourages him, and discourages him; it makes him stand,      30
and not stand. To conclude, drink tricks him right to
sleep—then lays him out and leaves him.

**MACDUFF**

I believe that drink laid you out last night.

**PORTER**

That it did, sir—it had me right by the throat. But I paid him back
for his trick, and I think I was too strong for him;             35
for even though he lifted me up by my legs, I still managed
to throw him up.

**MACDUFF**

Is your master awake?

> MACBETH *enters.*

Our knocking has awakened him. Here he comes.

**LENNOX**

Good morning, noble sir.                                           40

**MACBETH**

Good morning to you both.

**MACDUFF**

Is the King awake, worthy Thane?

**MACBETH**

Not yet.

**MACDUFF**

He did command me to call timely on him:

45 I have almost slipped the hour.

**MACBETH**

I'll bring you to him.

**MACDUFF**

I know this is a joyful trouble to you;

But yet 'tis one.

**MACBETH**

The labour we delight in physics pain.

50 This is the door.

**MACDUFF**

I'll make so bold to call,

For 'tis my limited service.

*Exit* MACDUFF.

**LENNOX**

Goes the King hence today?

**MACBETH**

He does: he did appoint so.

**LENNOX**

55 The night has been unruly. Where we lay,

Our chimneys were blown down, and, as they say,

Lamentings heard i' th' air, strange screams of death,

And prophesying with accents terrible

Of dire combustion and confused events

60 New hatch'd to th' woeful time. The obscure bird

**Clamour'd** the livelong night. Some say, the earth

Was feverous and did shake.

**MACBETH**

'Twas a rough night.

**LENNOX**

My young remembrance cannot parallel

65 A fellow to it.

*Enter* MACDUFF.

**MACDUFF**

O horror, horror, horror! Tongue nor heart

**MACDUFF**

He commanded me to call on him early:
I've almost missed the time. 45

**MACBETH**

I'll show you to him.

**MACDUFF**

I know this is a joyful trouble to you—
and yet it's still trouble.

**MACBETH**

The work we enjoy is a remedy for pain.
The door to Duncan's room is that way. 50

**MACDUFF**

I'll boldly call on him,
for it's my appointed duty.

     *MACDUFF exits.*

**LENNOX**

Is the King going away today?

**MACBETH**

Yes. He made commands for it.

**LENNOX**

The night was unruly. Where we slept, 55
chimneys were blown down; and it's said that
wailing was heard in the air—strange screams, like people dying.
And there were prophecies in terrible voices,
telling of dreadful uproars and troubling events,
about to make these days sorrowful. The owl 60
cried out the whole night through. Some say the earth
was feverish and shook.

**MACBETH**

It was a rough night.

**LENNOX**

In my young years, I can't remember one
to match it. 65

     *MACDUFF reenters.*

**MACDUFF**

Oh, horror, horror, horror! Neither my tongue nor my heart

Cannot conceive nor name thee!

**MACBETH AND LENNOX**
                                     What's the matter?

**MACDUFF**
   Confusion now hath made his masterpiece.
70 Most sacrilegious murder hath broke ope
   The Lord's anointed temple and stole thence
   The life o' th' building!

**MACBETH**
                              What is 't you say? The life?

**LENNOX**
   Mean you his Majesty?

**MACDUFF**
75 Approach the chamber and destroy your sight
   With a new Gorgon:* do not bid me speak;
   See, and then speak yourselves. Awake, awake!

         *Exeunt* MACBETH *and* LENNOX.

   Ring the alarum bell. Murder and treason!
   Banquo and Donalbain! Malcolm! Awake!
80 Shake off this downy sleep, death's counterfeit,
   And look on death itself! Up, up, and see
   The great doom's image! Malcolm! Banquo!
   As from your graves rise up, and walk like sprites,
   To countenance this horror. Ring the bell!

         *Bell rings. Enter* LADY [MACBETH].


**LADY MACBETH**
85 What's the business,
   That such a hideous trumpet calls to parley
   The sleepers of the house? Speak, speak!

**MACDUFF**
                                     O gentle lady,
   'Tis not for you to hear what I can speak:
90 The repetition, in a woman's ear,

---

76  *Gorgon* According to Greek mythology, the Gorgon was a monster, the sight of
which turned the beholder to stone.

can imagine or name you!

**MACBETH AND LENNOX**

What's the matter?

**MACDUFF**

Destruction has now made its masterpiece.
Most godless murder has broken open                          70
the Lord's holy temple and stolen from it
the life that was inside!

**MACBETH**

What are you saying? The life?

**LENNOX**

Do you mean his Majesty?

**MACDUFF**

Go to his bedroom and be blinded by the sight               75
of a new Gorgon. Do not ask me to speak.
Look—and then speak yourselves. Awake! Awake!

   *MACBETH and LENNOX exit.*

Ring the alarm bell. Murder and treason!
Banquo and Donalbain! Malcolm! Wake up!
Shake off your pleasant sleep, death's imitation,           80
and look at death itself! Get up, get up, and see
the Day of Judgment's likeness! Malcolm, Banquo,
rise up, as if from your graves, and walk like spirits,
in keeping with this horror. Ring the bell!

   *Bell rings.*

   *LADY MACBETH enters.*

**LADY MACBETH**

What's going on,                                            85
that such a hideous trumpet summons together
the people who sleep in this house? Tell me, tell me!

**MACDUFF**

Oh, gentle lady,
it's not right for you to hear what I have to tell.
To repeat it in a woman's ear                               90

Would murder as it fell.

*Enter* BANQUO.

                        O Banquo, Banquo,
Our royal master's murdered!

**LADY MACBETH**

                                Woe, alas!
95     What, in our house?

**BANQUO**

                     Too cruel anywhere.
Dear Duff, I prithee, contradict thyself,
And say it is not so.

*Enter* MACBETH, LENNOX, *and* ROSS.

**MACBETH**

     Had I but died an hour before this chance,
100    I had lived a blessed time; for from this instant
There's nothing serious in mortality:
All is but toys. Renown and grace is dead,
The wine of life is drawn, and the mere lees
Is left this vault to brag of.

*Enter* MALCOLM *and* DONALBAIN.

**DONALBAIN**

105    What is amiss?

**MACBETH**

                You are, and do not know 't.
The spring, the head, the fountain of your blood
Is stopp'd; the very source of it is stopp'd.

**MACDUFF**

     Your royal father's murdered.

**MALCOLM**

110                         O, by whom?

**LENNOX**

     Those of his chamber, as it seem'd, had done 't:
Their hands and faces were all badged with blood;
So were their daggers, which unwiped we found

would murder her as soon as she heard it.

BANQUO *enters.*

Oh, Banquo, Banquo,
Our royal master has been murdered!

**LADY MACBETH**
Woe, sorrow!
What, in our house?                                    95

**BANQUO**
Too cruel a thing to happen anywhere.
Dear Macduff, I beg you to contradict yourself
and say it isn't so.

MACBETH *and* LENNOX *reenter, with* ROSS.

**MACBETH**
If I had only died an hour before this happened,
I'd have lived a happy life; for after this moment,     100
there's nothing serious in human life.
All things are mere trifles. Fame and honor are dead.
The wine of life has been emptied, and only the dregs
are left for this world to brag about.

MALCOLM *and* DONALBAIN *enter.*

**DONALBAIN**
What's wrong?                                          105

**MACBETH**
You are, and do not know it.
The spring, the origin, the fountain of your blood
has been stopped; the very source of it has been stopped.

**MACDUFF**
Your royal father has been murdered.

**MALCOLM**
Oh, by whom?                                           110

**LENNOX**
It seems that the men in his chamber did it.
Their hands and faces were marked with blood.
So were their daggers, which we found unwiped

Upon their pillows. They stared and were distracted.
115 No man's life was to be trusted with them.

**MACBETH**
O, yet I do repent me of my fury,
That I did kill them.

**MACDUFF**
Wherefore did you so?

**MACBETH**
Who can be wise, amazed, **temp'rate** and furious,
120 Loyal and neutral, in a moment? No man.
The expedition of my violent love
Outrun the pauser, reason. Here lay Duncan,
His silver skin laced with his golden blood,
And his gashed stabs looked like a breach in nature
125 For ruin's wasteful entrance: there, the murderers,
Steeped in the colors of their trade, their daggers
Unmannerly breeched with gore. Who could refrain,
That had a heart to love, and in that heart
Courage to make's love known?

**LADY MACBETH**
Help me hence, ho!
130

**MACDUFF**
Look to the lady.

**MALCOLM** [*aside to* DONALBAIN]
Why do we hold our tongues,
That most may claim this argument for ours?

**DONALBAIN** [*aside to* MALCOLM]
What should be spoken here, where our fate,
135 Hid in an auger-hole, may rush and seize us?
Let's away. Our tears are not yet brewed.

**MALCOLM** [*aside to* DONALBAIN]
Nor our strong sorrow upon the foot of motion.

**BANQUO**
Look to the lady.

[LADY MACBETH *is carried out.*]

upon their pillows. They stared and seemed bewildered.
No man's life was to be trusted with them.                           115

**MACBETH**
Oh, and yet I regret that I killed them
in my fury.

**MACDUFF**
Why did you do so?

**MACBETH**
Who can be wise and bewildered, calm and furious,
loyal and neutral, all at the same time? No man.                     120
The haste of my intense love
outran my more cautious rationality. Here lay Duncan,
his silver skin streaked with his golden blood;
and his gaping wounds looked like an opening in the world
to let in wasteful destruction. There were the murderers,            125
drenched in the color of their trade, their daggers
improperly clothed in gore. Who could stop himself
if he had a loving heart—and if he had courage
in that heart to act on his love?

**LADY MACBETH** (*fainting*)
Help me away, oh!                                                    130

**MACDUFF**
Help the lady.

**MALCOLM** (*aside to* DONALBAIN)
Why do we keep quiet,
since we're the ones most concerned with this topic?

**DONALBAIN** (*aside to* MALCOLM)
What can we say here,
where our doom might rush out                                        135
from the smallest hiding place to seize us? Let's go away;
our tears are not ready yet.

**MALCOLM** (*aside to* DONALBAIN)
Nor is our deep sorrow
ready to be expressed in action.

**BANQUO**
Help the lady.                                                       140

LADY MACBETH *is carried out.*

And when we have our naked frailties hid,
140  That suffer in exposure, let us meet
And question this most bloody piece of work,
To know it further. Fears and scruples shake us.
In the great hand of God I stand, and thence
Against the undivulged **pretense** I fight
145  Of treasonous **malice**.

**MACDUFF**

And so do I.

**ALL**

So all.

**MACBETH**

Let's briefly put on manly readiness,
And meet i' th' hall together.

**ALL**

150  Well contented.

*Exeunt [all but* MALCOLM *and* DONALBAIN].

**MALCOLM**

What will you do? Let's not **consort** with them.
To show an unfelt sorrow is an office
Which the false man does easy. I'll to England.

**DONALBAIN**

To Ireland, I; our separated fortune
155  Shall keep us both the safer. Where we are,
There's daggers in men's smiles. The near in blood,
The nearer bloody.

**MALCOLM**

This murderous shaft that's shot
Hath not yet lighted, and our safest way
160  Is to avoid the aim. Therefore, to horse!
And let us not be dainty of leave-taking,
But shift away. There's warrant in that theft
Which steals itself when there's no mercy left.

*Exeunt.*

And after we have clothed our half-naked bodies,
which now are at risk from the cold, let us meet
and examine this bloody piece of work,
and try to understand it better. We are shaken by fears and
    doubts.
I place myself in the hands of God; relying on Him,
I shall fight against this treasonous cruelty,
the purpose of which is still unknown.

145

**MACDUFF**
And so shall I.

**ALL**
So shall we all.

**MACBETH**
Let's quickly put on our armor
and meet together in the hall.

**ALL**
We all agree.

150

      *All but* MALCOLM *and* DONALBAIN *exit.*

**MALCOLM**
What will you do? Let's not meet with them.
To show an unfelt sorrow is a duty
that comes easily to false-faced men. I'll go to England.

**DONALBAIN**
I'll go to Ireland. By going our separate ways
we'll both be safer. Wherever we are,

155

men's smiles have daggers in them. The closer the relation,
the more likely we are to be killed.

**MALCOLM**
This murderous arrow that's been shot
has not yet struck, and it's safest for us
to stay out of its path. So let's mount our horses,

160

and let's not be fussy about farewells,
but sneak away. It's justifiable theft
to steal oneself away from such a dangerous situation.

    *They exit.*

# ACT II, SCENE IV

[*Outside Macbeth's castle.*] *Enter* ROSS *with an* OLD MAN.

**OLD MAN**

Threescore and ten I can remember well:
Within the volume of which time I have seen
Hours dreadful and things strange, but this sore night
Hath trifled former knowings.

**ROSS**

5                                          Ha, good father,
Thou seest the heavens, as troubled with man's act,
Threatens his bloody stage. By th' clock, 'tis day,
And yet dark night strangles the traveling lamp:
Is 't night's predominance, or the day's shame,
10      That darkness does the face of earth entomb,
When living light should kiss it?

**OLD MAN**

                                          'Tis unnatural,
Even like the deed that's done. On Tuesday last
A falcon,* tow'ring in her pride of place,
15      Was by a mousing owl hawked at and killed.

**ROSS**

And Duncan's horses—a thing most strange and certain—
Beauteous and swift, the minions of their race,
Turn'd wild in nature, broke their stalls, flung out,
Contending 'gainst obedience, as they would make
20      War with mankind.

**OLD MAN**

                                          'Tis said they ate each other.

**ROSS**

They did so, to th' amazement of mine eyes
That look'd upon 't.

---

14   *falcon* any of various hawks used for hunting in the sport of hawking, or
falconry, in which birds were trained to pursue and attack wild fowl or game

# ACT 2, SCENE 4

*Outside Macbeth's castle.* ROSS *and an* OLD MAN *enter.*

**OLD MAN**
I can remember seventy years well,
and in all that time I have seen
dreadful hours and strange things; but this terrible night
makes all I've seen seem trivial by comparison.

**ROSS**
Ah, good father, 5
you see how the heavens, as if troubled by man's deeds,
threaten his world. It's day according to the clock,
and yet the dark night keeps out the sun.
Is it because the night is strong, or because the day is ashamed,
that darkness entombs the face of the earth 10
when living light should kiss it?

**OLD MAN**
It's unnatural,
just like the deed that's been done. Last Tuesday
a falcon, while soaring at her greatest height,
was attacked and killed by an owl that normally hunts
only mice. 15

**ROSS**
And here's something strange but true: Duncan's beautiful, swift
horses—
the finest of their breed—
went completely wild, broke out of their stalls and ran loose,
defying all attempts to control them; it was as if they wanted
to make war with mankind. 20

**OLD MAN**
It's said that they ate each other.

**ROSS**
They did, and my eyes were bewildered
to see it.

*Enter* MACDUFF.

Here comes the good Macduff.

25 How goes the world, sir, now?

**MACDUFF**

Why, see you not?

**ROSS**

Is 't known who did this more than bloody deed?

**MACDUFF**

Those that Macbeth hath slain.

**ROSS**

Alas, the day!

30 What good could they pretend?

**MACDUFF**

They were **suborned**:

Malcolm and Donalbain, the King's two sons,
Are stol'n away and fled, which puts upon them
Suspicion of the deed.

**ROSS**

35 'Gainst nature still!

Thriftless ambition, that wilt ravin up
Thine own life's means! Then 'tis most like
The sovereignty will fall upon Macbeth.

**MACDUFF**

He is already named, and gone to Scone*
40 To be invested.

**ROSS**

Where is Duncan's body?

**MACDUFF**

Carried to Colmekill,*
The sacred storehouse of his predecessors
And guardian of their bones.

**ROSS**

45 Will you to Scone?

---

39  *Scone*  ancient capital, near Perth, where the kings of Scotland were crowned

42  *Colmekill*  island cell of St. Columba, now known as Iona, where Scottish kings were buried

*MACDUFF enters.*

Here comes the good Macduff.
How's the world going now, sir?                                    25

**MACDUFF**
Why, can't you see?

**ROSS**
Is it known who did this more than bloody deed?

**MACDUFF**
The men that Macbeth has killed.

**ROSS**
Sorrowful day!
What could they expect to gain from it?                            30

**MACDUFF**
They were bribed.
Malcolm and Donalbain, the King's two sons,
have sneaked away and fled; this puts suspicion of the deed
against them.

**ROSS**
Even more unnatural!                                               35
What wasteful ambition, to greedily devour
the source of their own lives! Then it's very likely
that royal power will go to Macbeth.

**MACDUFF**
He's already been chosen, and has gone to Scone
to be made King.                                                   40

**ROSS**
Where is Duncan's body?

**MACDUFF**
It's been taken to Colmekill,
the sacred tomb of past kings,
and the protector of their bones.

**ROSS**
Will you go to Scone?                                              45

**MACDUFF**

No, cousin, I'll to Fife.*

**ROSS**

Well, I will thither.

**MACDUFF**

Well, may you see things well done there. Adieu,
Lest our old robes sit easier than our new!

**ROSS**

50      Farewell, father.

**OLD MAN**

God's benison go with you, and with those
That would make good of bad and friends of foes.

*Exeunt omnes.*

---

46    *Fife* in eastern Scotland. Macduff chooses to go to his own castle rather than to
Scone and the coronation.

**MACDUFF**

No, cousin, I'll go to Fife.

**ROSS**

Well, I'll go there.

**MACDUFF**

Well, I hope you'll see things well done there—
or else we'll long for the days of Duncan's rule! Good-bye!

**ROSS**

Good-bye, father.

50

**OLD MAN**

May God's blessing go with you—and with all others
that seek to make good out of bad and friends out of foes.

*They exit.*

# Act II Review

## Discussion Questions

1. What is the significance of the dagger in Scene i?

2. Why does Lady Macbeth faint?

3. Why does Shakespeare begin Scene i in Act II with Banquo and Fleance? Decide what purpose this scene serves dramatically.

4. In Act II, Scene ii, Lady Macbeth says, "The attempt and not the deed" itself will ruin her and Macbeth. What do you think would happen if the attempt to kill Duncan or the cover-up failed?

5. What goes wrong with Lady Macbeth's plan, and how does she fix the situation? Explain why she needs to correct the error.

6. The killing of King Duncan does not occur onstage. Why do you think Shakespeare chooses not to show his death?

7. Do you think Macbeth would have gone ahead with the murder of Duncan if his wife had not encouraged him to do so? Explain your answer.

8. Do you think Macduff believes that Malcolm and Donalbain were responsible for the death of their father? Discuss your answer.

## Literary Elements

1. Give some reasons why **comic relief** such as the Porter scene can be found in a tragedy like *Macbeth*.

2. A **double entendre** is a statement that has two different meanings, one of which is often sexual. Find an example of double entendre in the Porter's speech on pages 86–88.

3.  **Double entendres** can also be used for darker purposes. What two interpretations can you give to the line "Macbeth does murder sleep" (Act II, Scene ii, line 45)?

4.  Good drama has **conflict**: struggle between opposing forces. **External conflict** refers to a struggle between individuals and outside forces or other individuals. **Internal conflict** refers to a mental or emotional struggle within the individual. Find examples of both kinds of conflict in the first two acts.

# Writing Prompts

1.  Pretend you are a journalist covering a crime beat. After investigating the crime scene and interviewing all the key players at Macbeth's castle, write your news story. Remember to answer the questions who, what, where, and when and to include quotes from the various characters.

2.  Choose a quotation from one of the scenes in Act II that you feel best characterizes that scene. In a paragraph, discuss why you think this quotation is significant and effective at conveying the events or emotions of this scene.

3.  Write a dialogue telling what happened at the meeting where Macbeth was elected to be the new king. Was there dissension? Were other candidates considered?

4.  Compose a letter from Malcolm to Donalbain or vice versa after the brothers have escaped to England and Ireland respectively. Use the language of Shakespeare's day in writing the letter.

# Macbeth
## ACT III

John Gielgud, as Macbeth, sees the ghost of Banquo, played by Leon Quartermaine.
Piccadilly Theatre, 1942

"It will have blood, they say;
blood will have blood."

# Before You Read

1. Think about how Macbeth makes decisions. Then compare the way you make important decisions with Macbeth's decision-making style.

2. How do you think the Macbeths will enjoy their new status?

3. At this point, what is your opinion of Macbeth? Of Lady Macbeth? Describe their relationship.

# Literary Elements

1. **Verse structure** refers to the rhythm and rhyme scheme of the language of the play. Shakespeare uses both rhyming and unrhymed verse in his plays. Iambic pentameter consists of an unaccented syllable followed by an accented syllable, with five beats, or accents, in each measured line. A good example is Macbeth's speech in Act I, Scene iii: "So foul and fair a day I have not seen."

2. An **implication** is a hint or suggestion contained in the writing. In Act I, Scene iii, Macbeth says his "Present fears / Are less than horrible imaginings." Here he implies that knowing what to fear is better than not knowing what to fear and having to imagine it.

3. An **allusion** is a reference to a historical or literary figure, happening, or event that is meant to enhance the meaning of the story. In Act II, Scene ii, Macbeth refers to Neptune, the Roman god of the sea, when expressing fear that his murderous conscience will never be cleansed. "Will all great Neptune's ocean wash this blood / Clean from my hand?"

# Words to Know

The following vocabulary words appear in Act III in the original text of Shakespeare's play. However, they are words that are still commonly used. Read the definitions here and pay attention to the words as you read the play (they will be in boldfaced type).

| | |
|---|---|
| **assailable** | vulnerable; open to attack |
| **blanched** | whitened; paled |
| **dauntless** | fearless; unafraid |
| **disposition** | personality; character |
| **incensed** | enraged; infuriated |
| **indissoluble** | firm; unbreakable |
| **infirmity** | illness; sickness |
| **jocund** | cheerful; affable |
| **malevolence** | ill will; spite |
| **mirth** | jollity; gaiety |
| **posterity** | heirs; future generations |
| **purged** | eliminated; cleansed |
| **rancor** [rancors] | bitterness; hostility |
| **rebuked** | scolded; reprimanded |

# Act Summary

The Witches' second prediction has come true: Macbeth and Lady Macbeth are now King and Queen of Scotland.

But Macbeth is troubled. He rightly guesses that Banquo suspects him of the murder. Moreover, the Witches predicted that Banquo's descendants would become kings. So Macbeth decides to do away with both Banquo and his son, Fleance.

Macbeth persuades some men to meet Banquo and Fleance on a road and murder them both. The Murderers kill Banquo, but Fleance escapes.

That very night, Macbeth holds a feast. The First Murderer slips into the hall and lets Macbeth know that Banquo is dead and Fleance still at

Macbeth, center, played by Christopher Walken, speaks to the Murderers.
The New York Shakespeare Festival, 1974

large. Macbeth pretends to fault Banquo for not attending his banquet when who should show up but Banquo's bloody ghost, sitting at the banquet table!

Macbeth panics and rages at the ghost, which nobody else sees. Once the ghost has disappeared, Lady Macbeth persuades the banquet guests to go home. Macbeth wonders why Macduff has not attended the banquet and plans to find out more from the spies he has employed. His ravings have convinced some of his subjects that he's a murderer.

Meanwhile, Duncan's son Malcolm has fled to England. There he seeks military aid from the English King Edward to overthrow Macbeth.

Constantly fearing plots against him, Macbeth rules the kingdom with an iron fist. Scotland is ready to explode into civil war. Desperate for advice, Macbeth seeks out the Witches in their lair.

# ACT III, SCENE I

[*Forres. The palace.*] *Enter BANQUO.*

**BANQUO**
Thou hast it now—King, Cawdor, Glamis, all,
As the Weïrd Women promised, and, I fear,
Thou play'dst most foully for 't. Yet it was said
It should not stand in thy **posterity**,
5    But that myself should be the root and father
Of many kings. If there come truth from them—
As upon thee, Macbeth, their speeches shine—
Why, by the verities on thee made good,
May they not be my oracles as well
10   And set me up in hope? But hush, no more!

*Sennet sounded. Enter MACBETH, as King,*
*LADY [MACBETH], LENNOX, ROSS, LORDS,*
*and ATTENDANTS.*

**MACBETH**
Here's our chief guest.

**LADY MACBETH**
               If he had been forgotten,
It had been as a gap in our great feast,
And all-thing unbecoming.

**MACBETH**
15   Tonight we hold a solemn supper, sir,
And I'll request your presence.

**BANQUO**
                  Let your Highness
Command upon me, to the which my duties
Are with a most **indissoluble** tie
20   Forever knit.

**MACBETH**
Ride you this afternoon?

**BANQUO**
             Ay, my good lord.

# ACT 3, SCENE 1

*Forres. The palace.* BANQUO *enters.*

**BANQUO**
You've got it all now—King, Thane of Cawdor, Thane of Glamis,
  everything—
just as the Witches promised; and I'm afraid
you did something extremely wicked to get it. Still, they said
that the throne wouldn't stay in your family,
but that I would be the ancestor and father                                  5
of many kings. If what they say is true
(and their promises have been glowingly fulfilled for you,
  Macbeth)—
why, judging from all that you've gained,
mightn't they be my fortune-tellers as well,
and give me reason to hope? But hush, I must be quiet.                        10

*Trumpet call.* MACBETH *and* LADY MACBETH *enter as King and
Queen, accompanied by* LENNOX, ROSS, LORDS, *and*
SERVANTS.

**MACBETH**
Here's our most important guest.

**LADY MACBETH**
If he had been forgotten,
there would have been a gap in our great feast
which would be completely improper.

**MACBETH**
Tonight we hold a formal supper, sir,                                        15
and I ask you to be there.

**BANQUO**
Let your highness
command me, for my duties
are forever bound to you
by an unbreakable tie.                                                       20

**MACBETH**
Will you be riding this afternoon?

**BANQUO**
Yes, my good lord.

**MACBETH**

We should have else desired your good advice,
Which still hath been both grave and prosperous,
25   In this day's council; but we'll take tomorrow.
Is 't far you ride?

**BANQUO**

As far, my lord, as will fill up the time
'Twixt this and supper. Go not my horse the better,
I must become a borrower of the night
30   For a dark hour or twain.

**MACBETH**

                                        Fail not our feast.

**BANQUO**

My lord, I will not.

**MACBETH**

We hear our bloody cousins are bestowed
In England and in Ireland, not confessing
35   Their cruel parricide, filling their hearers
With strange invention. But of that tomorrow,
When therewithal we shall have cause of state
Craving us jointly. Hie you to horse. Adieu,
Till you return at night. Goes Fleance with you?

**BANQUO**

40   Ay, my good lord. Our time does call upon's.

**MACBETH**

I wish your horses swift and sure of foot;
And so I do commend you to their backs.
Farewell.

        *Exit* BANQUO.

Let every man be master of this time
45   Till seven at night. To make society
The sweeter welcome, we will keep ourself
Till supper-time alone. While then, God be with you!

        *Exeunt* LORDS [*and all but* MACBETH *and a*
        SERVANT].

Sirrah, a word with you: attend those men
Our pleasure?

**MACBETH**

Otherwise, we would have asked for your good advice
(which has always been both well-considered and helpful)
in today's council meeting; but you'll be there tomorrow.          25
Are you riding far?

**BANQUO**

Far enough, my lord, to fill up the time
between now and supper. Unless my horse runs faster than usual,
I'll have to be riding at night
while it's dark for an hour or two.          30

**MACBETH**

Don't miss our feast.

**BANQUO**

My lord, I will not.

**MACBETH**

We hear that our murderous cousins have gone
to England and Ireland. They haven't confessed
their cruel murder of their father and are filling people's ears          35
with strange lies. But more about that tomorrow,
when state business also will demand
both of our attention. Go, to your horse. Good-bye,
until you return tonight. Is Fleance going with you?

**BANQUO**

Yes, my good lord. Time is short, and we must go.          40

**MACBETH**

I hope your horses are swift and sure-footed;
and so I entrust you to their backs. Farewell.

> BANQUO *exits.*

Every man may do as he likes
until seven tonight. To make your company          45
even more welcome, we will keep to ourselves
until supper time, alone. Till then, God be with you.

> *All exit except* MACBETH *and a* SERVANT.

Sirrah, a word with you. Are those men waiting
to see us?

**SERVANT**

50     They are, my lord, without the palace gate.

**MACBETH**

Bring them before us.

        *Exit* SERVANT.

                To be thus is nothing,
But to be safely thus. Our fears in Banquo
Stick deep, and in his royalty of nature
55     Reigns that which would be feared. 'Tis much he dares;
And, to that **dauntless** temper of his mind,
He hath a wisdom that doth guide his valour
To act in safety. There is none but he
Whose being I do fear; and under him,
60     My genius is **rebuked**, as it is said
Mark Antony's was by Caesar. He chid the Sisters
When first they put the name of King upon me,
And bade them speak to him. Then prophet-like
They hailed him father to a line of kings.
65     Upon my head they placed a fruitless crown,
And put a barren scepter* in my gripe,
Thence to be wrenched with an unlineal hand,
No son of mine succeeding. If 't be so,
For Banquo's issue have I filed my mind;
70     For them the gracious Duncan have I murdered;
Put **rancors** in the vessel of my peace
Only for them, and mine eternal jewel
Given to the common enemy of man,
To make them kings, the seed of Banquo kings!
75     Rather than so, come fate into the list.
And champion me to th' utterance!*—Who's there!

        *Enter* SERVANT *and two* MURDERERS.

---

66   *scepter* a staff or baton carried by a sovereign that signifies royal authority

76   *champion me to th' utterance* fight to the utmost or extremity. *Utterance* derives
from the French "à l'outrance," a chivalric term meaning combat to the death.

**SERVANT**

They are, my lord; they're outside the palace gate.    50

**MACBETH**

Bring them to us.

　　　SERVANT *exits.*

To be king is useless,
unless one is safely king. My fears of Banquo
run deep, and his regal character
is something that I should fear. He dares to do much—    55
and although he is of a bold temperament,
he also has wisdom, which guides him to act safely
even in boldness. There is no one but him
whose existence I fear, and my guardian spirit
is intimidated by him, as it is said    60
Mark Antony's was by Caesar. He scolded the Witches
when they first called me by the name of King,
and demanded that they speak to him. Then, prophet-like,
they declared him father to a line of kings.
They placed a profitless crown on my head    65
and put a barren scepter in my grip—
to be yanked away by someone not of my family,
since no son of mine will succeed me. If this is true,
I have corrupted my mind to help Banquo's offspring;
for them I have murdered the most kindly Duncan;    70
I have lost my peace of mind and gained trouble,
just for them; and I have given my immortal soul
to the devil,
to make them kings—the offspring of Banquo, kings!
Rather than have that happen, let fate come to the field of
　　combat    75
and fight me to the death.—Who's there?

　　　SERVANT *reenters, with two* MURDERERS.

[*to* SERVANT] Now go to the door, and stay there till we call.

    *Exit* SERVANT.

Was it not yesterday we spoke together?

**FIRST MURDERER**
It was, so please your Highness.

**MACBETH**
<br>80                                 Well then, now
Have you considered of my speeches? Know
That it was he in the times past, which held you
So under fortune, which you thought had been
Our innocent self. This I made good to you
<br>85   In our last conference, passed in probation with you,
How you were borne in hand, how cross'd, the instruments,
Who wrought with them, and all things else that might
To half a soul and to a notion crazed
Say "Thus did Banquo."

**FIRST MURDERER**
<br>90                       You made it known to us.

**MACBETH**
I did so, and went further, which is now
Our point of second meeting. Do you find
Your patience so predominant in your nature
That you can let this go? Are you so gospeled,
<br>95   To pray for this good man and for his issue,
Whose heavy hand hath bowed you to the grave
And beggared yours forever?

**FIRST MURDERER**
                     We are men, my liege.

**MACBETH**
Ay, in the catalogue ye go for men,
<br>100  As hounds and greyhounds, mongrels, spaniels, curs,
Shoughs, water-rugs and demi-wolves are clept
All by the name of dogs. The valued file
Distinguishes the swift, the slow, the subtle,
The housekeeper, the hunter, every one
<br>105  According to the gift which bounteous nature
Hath in him closed, whereby he does receive

(*to* SERVANT) Now go to the door, and wait there till we call you.

SERVANT *exits*.

Wasn't it yesterday when we spoke together?

**FIRST MURDERER**

It was, may it please your Highness.

**MACBETH**

Well then,                                                                    80
have you thought over what I told you? Remember
that it was Banquo who kept good fortune away from you
in the past; you thought that I had done so,
but I was innocent. I explained this to you
at our last meeting, carefully proving to you                                85
how you were deceived and hindered, the means
used to do it, and everything else that would convince
even a half-wit or a madman,
"This is what Banquo did!"

**FIRST MURDERER**

You made it known to us.                                                      90

**MACBETH**

I did, and I went further—which is now
the point of our second meeting. Do you find
that patience is so strong a part of your character
that you can let this go? Are you so meekly Christian
that you'd pray for this good man and his offspring,                         95
even after his heavy hand has pushed you toward the grave
and made your offspring beggars forever?

**FIRST MURDERER**

We are only mortal men, my lord.

**MACBETH**

Yes, in a casual list you pass for men,
just as hounds, greyhounds, mongrels, spaniels, curs,                       100
shoughs, water-rugs, and demi-wolves are all called
by the name of dogs. The list that shows value
distinguishes the swift, the slow, the sly,
the watchdog, the hunter—every one
according to the gift which generous nature                                 105
has given him; in such a list, each dog receives

Particular addition, from the bill
That writes them all alike: and so of men.
Now, if you have a station in the file,
110    Not i' th' worst rank of manhood, say 't,
And I will put that business in your bosoms,
Whose execution takes your enemy off,
Grapples you to the heart and love of us,
Who wear our health but sickly in his life,
115    Which in his death were perfect.

**SECOND MURDERER**

                            I am one, my liege,
Whom the vile blows and buffets of the world
Have so **incensed** that I am reckless what
I do to spite the world.

**FIRST MURDERER**

120                     And I another
So weary with disasters, tugged with fortune,
That I would set my life on any chance,
To mend it, or be rid on 't.

**MACBETH**

                     Both of you
125    Know Banquo was your enemy.

**BOTH MURDERERS**

                       True, my lord.

**MACBETH**

So is he mine, and in such bloody distance
That every minute of his being thrusts
Against my near'st of life. And though I could
130    With barefaced power sweep him from my sight
And bid my will avouch it, yet I must not,
For certain friends that are both his and mine,
Whose loves I may not drop, but wail his fall
Who I myself struck down. And thence it is,
135    That I to your assistance do make love,
Masking the business from the common eye
For sundry weighty reasons.

a special distinction not to be found in a list
that shows all dogs as the same. And this is true of men.
Now, if you have a place in the list
above the lowest rank of manhood, tell me;                           110
and I will assign you a task which,
once it is done, will rid you of your enemy
and attach you to my heart with love;
for while he lives, my health is sickly—
but if he were dead, it would be perfect.                            115

**SECOND MURDERER**
My lord, I am a man
so angered by the vicious blows
and beatings of the world, I don't care what
I do to get back at the world.

**FIRST MURDERER**
And I am another man                                                 120
so weary of disasters, so knocked about by fortune,
that I would risk my life in any way
to mend it or be rid of it.

**MACBETH**
You both
know that Banquo is your enemy.                                      125

**BOTH MURDERERS**
True, my lord.

**MACBETH**
He's also mine—and my hatred is so bloody,
that every minute he lives is a stab
at my very heart. And though I could
openly use my power to sweep him from my sight                       130
and justify it as my royal will, I must not,
because of certain friends we have in common
whose affection I can't afford to lose; I must appear to mourn
the death of the man who I myself killed. And this is why
I woo you to come to my aid:                                         135
I must hide the deed from the common eye
for several important reasons.

**SECOND MURDERER**
　　　　　　　　　　　We shall, my lord,
　　Perform what you command us.

**FIRST MURDERER**
　　　　　　　　　　　　　　Though our lives—

**MACBETH**
　　Your spirits shine through you. Within this hour at most
　　I will advise you where to plant yourselves,
　　Acquaint you with the perfect spy o' th' time,*
　　The moment on 't; for 't must be done tonight,
　　And something from the palace; always thought
　　That I require a clearness. And with him—
　　To leave no rubs nor botches in the work—
　　Fleance his son, that keeps him company,
　　Whose absence is no less material to me
　　Than is his father's, must embrace the fate
　　Of that dark hour. Resolve yourselves apart:
　　I'll come to you anon.

**MURDERERS**
　　　　　　　　　　We are resolved, my lord.

**MACBETH**
　　I'll call upon you straight. Abide within.

　　　　*Exeunt* MURDERERS.

　　It is concluded: Banquo, thy soul's flight,
　　If it find heaven, must find it out tonight.

　　　　*Exit.*

---

143　*perfect . . . time*　the very moment when to do it

**SECOND MURDERER**

    My lord, we shall
    do what you command us.

**FIRST MURDERER**

    Even if our lives—                           140

**MACBETH**

    Now you show your true spirit. In less than an hour,
    I'll tell you where to plant yourselves
    and give you the best information available
    concerning when to do it—for it must be done tonight,
    and at some distance from the palace; always remember    145
    that I mustn't be implicated. And in order
    that the job not be botched or bungled,
    Fleance, his son, who keeps him company
    (and whose absence is just as important to me
    as that of his father) must meet the same fate    150
    at that dark hour. Go away and make up your minds
    I'll come to you soon.

**BOTH MURDERERS**

    We've made up our minds, my lord.

**MACBETH**

    I'll call upon you immediately. Wait inside.

        MURDERERS *exit.*

    It is agreed upon. Banquo, if your soul    155
    is going to fly to heaven, it must find its way there tonight.

        MACBETH *exits.*

# ACT III, SCENE II

*[The palace.] Enter* LADY MACBETH *and a* SERVANT.

**LADY MACBETH**

Is Banquo gone from court?

**SERVANT**

Ay, madam, but returns again tonight.

**LADY MACBETH**

Say to the King, I would attend his leisure
For a few words.

**SERVANT**

               Madam, I will.

5

*Exit.*

**LADY MACBETH**

                    Nought's had, all's spent,
Where our desire is got without content:
'Tis safer to be that which we destroy
Than by destruction dwell in doubtful joy.

*Enter* MACBETH.

10 How now, my lord! Why do you keep alone,
Of sorriest fancies your companions making,
Using those thoughts which should indeed have died
With them they think on? Things without all remedy
Should be without regard: what's done is done.

**MACBETH**

15 We have scorched the snake, not kill'd it:
She'll close and be herself, whilst our poor malice
Remains in danger of her former tooth.
But let the frame of things disjoint, both the worlds suffer,
Ere we will eat our meal in fear, and sleep
20 In the affliction of these terrible dreams
That shake us nightly. Better be with the dead,
Whom we, to gain our peace, have sent to peace,
Than on the torture of the mind to lie
In restless ecstasy. Duncan is in his grave;

# ACT 3, SCENE 2

*The palace.* LADY MACBETH *and a* SERVANT *enter.*

**LADY MACBETH**
Has Banquo gone away from court?

**SERVANT**
Yes, madam—but he returns again tonight.

**LADY MACBETH**
Tell the King that I await his convenience
to have a few words with him.

**SERVANT**
Madam, I will.                                                                5

SERVANT *exits.*

**LADY MACBETH**
Nothing's gained, and everything's lost,
when we've got everything we desired but remain uneasy.
It would be better to be the one we murdered
than to live in uncertain joy because of our murder.

MACBETH *enters.*

Tell me, my lord—why do you stay alone,                          10
keeping company only with your most wretched musings,
entertaining thoughts that really should have died
along with him you think about? Things that can't be changed
should be ignored. What's done is done.

**MACBETH**
We've only cut the snake, not killed it.                            15
She'll heal and be herself again, and our feeble hatred
will remain endangered by her tooth, just as before.
But let the universe crash down, and let both heaven and earth
    perish,
before we will eat our meals in fear, or have our sleep
plagued with these terrible dreams                                  20
that disturb us nightly. We'd be better off joining the dead,
whom we have sent to their peace in attempting to gain our
    own peace,
than to have to suffer upon the rack of the mind
in restless frenzy. Duncan is in his grave.

25 After life's fitful fever he sleeps well.
Treason has done his worst. Nor steel, nor poison,
Malice domestic, foreign levy, nothing,
Can touch him further.

**LADY MACBETH**
                            Come on.
30 Gentle my lord, sleek o'er your rugged looks;
Be bright and jovial among your guests tonight.

**MACBETH**
So shall I, love; and so, I pray, be you.
Let your remembrance apply to Banquo;
Present him eminence, both with eye and tongue:
35 Unsafe the while, that we must lave
Our honours in these flattering streams,
And make our faces vizards to our hearts,
Disguising what they are.

**LADY MACBETH**
                            You must leave this.

**MACBETH**
40 O, full of scorpions is my mind, dear wife!
Thou know'st that Banquo, and his Fleance, lives.

**LADY MACBETH**
But in them nature's copy's not eterne.

**MACBETH**
There's comfort yet; they are **assailable**.
Then be thou **jocund**. Ere the bat hath flown
45 His cloistered flight, ere to black Hecate's summons
The shard-borne* beetle with his drowsy hums
Hath rung night's yawning peal, there shall be done
A deed of dreadful note.

**LADY MACBETH**
                            What's to be done?

**MACBETH**
50 Be innocent of the knowledge, dearest chuck,

---

46    *shard-borne* carried aloft on scaly wings (wings resembling shards of pottery)

After life's fitful fever, he sleeps well.　　　　　　　25
Treason has done its worst to him. Neither steel, poison,
rebellion, foreign troops, nor anything else
can bother him anymore.

**LADY MACBETH**

Come on with me.
My noble lord, smooth over your furrowed expression.　　30
Be cheerful and friendly with your guests tonight.

**MACBETH**

I shall, love—and please, you do the same.
Give special attention to Banquo;
honor him well with both your eye and tongue.
You and I are unsafe as long as we　　　　　　　35
must wash our honors in streams of flattery,
and turn our faces into masks to disguise
what our hearts really are.

**LADY MACBETH**

You mustn't think about this.

**MACBETH**

Oh, my brain is full of scorpions, dear wife!　　　　　40
You know that Banquo and his son Fleance are alive.

**LADY MACBETH**

But nature hasn't given them an eternal lease on life.

**MACBETH**

There's some comfort in that; they can be attacked.
So be merry. Before the bat has flown
his blind flight, and before the lazily humming, scaly winged
　　　beetle,
at black Hecate's command, has rung the bell　　　　45
that brings on nightly slumber, a most dreadful deed
will be done.

**LADY MACBETH**

What are you going to do?

**MACBETH**

Keep your innocence by not knowing about it, dearest darling,　50

Till thou applaud the deed. Come, seeling* night,
Scarf up the tender eye of pitiful day,
And with thy bloody and invisible hand
Cancel and tear to pieces that great bond*
55 Which keeps me pale! Light thickens, and the crow
Makes wing to th' rooky wood.*
Good things of day begin to droop and drowse,
While night's black agents to their preys do rouse.
Thou marvel'st at my words, but hold thee still;
60 Things bad begun make strong themselves by ill.
So, prithee, go with me.

     *Exeunt.*

---

51   *seeling* In falconry, to "seel" was to sew up the eyelids of a hawk to help in taming the bird.

54   *cancel . . . bond* cancel the obligations of loyalty and love that a king has to his subjects and more generally that human beings have to one another

56   *rooky wood* a woods full of rooks, black birds about the size of crows

until you can applaud the deed. Come, blinding night;
cover up the tender eye of merciful day,
and with your unseen, murderous hand
cancel and tear to pieces Banquo and Fleance's lease on life,
for it frightens me. Daylight grows dim, and the crow          55
flies to the dark and dismal woods.
The wholesome things of day begin to droop and sleep,
while night's troublesome creatures are waking to hunt their prey.
You are amazed by my words, but keep quiet.
Things with evil beginnings become stronger by more evil.        60
So please—come along with me.

    *They exit.*

# ACT III, SCENE III

[*Near the palace.*] *Enter three* MURDERERS.

**FIRST MURDERER**
But who did bid thee join with us?

**THIRD MURDERER**
                                        Macbeth.

**SECOND MURDERER**
He needs not our mistrust, since he delivers
Our offices and what we have to do
5    To the direction just.

**FIRST MURDERER**
                                Then stand with us.
The west yet glimmers with some streaks of day.
Now spurs the lated traveler apace
To gain the timely inn, and near approaches
10   The subject of our watch.

**THIRD MURDERER**
                                Hark! I hear horses.

**BANQUO** [*within*]
Give us a light there, ho!

**SECOND MURDERER**
                                Then 'tis he. The rest
That are within the note of expectation
15   Already are i' th' court.

**FIRST MURDERER**
                                His horses go about.

**THIRD MURDERER**
Almost a mile; but he does usually—
So all men do—from hence to th' palace gate
Make it their walk.

**SECOND MURDERER**
20   A light, a light!

# ACT 3, SCENE 3

*A park or lawn, with a gate leading to the palace. Three MURDERERS enter.*

**FIRST MURDERER**
But who asked you to join us?

**THIRD MURDERER**
Macbeth.

**SECOND MURDERER** *(to FIRST MURDERER)*
We needn't mistrust him, since he's able to describe
our job and what we have to do
down to the smallest detail.                                        5

**FIRST MURDERER** *(to THIRD MURDERER)*
Then wait here with us.
There is still a glimmer in the west, with streaks of day.
Some belated traveler is now spurring his horse
to get to an inn before dark, and the person we await
is approaching.                                                     10

**THIRD MURDERER**
Listen—I hear horses.

**BANQUO** *(offstage to a SERVANT)*
Give me a light, quickly!

**SECOND MURDERER**
Then it's Banquo. The rest
of those on the list of expected guests
are already at the court.                                           15

**FIRST MURDERER**
His servants are taking his horses.

**THIRD MURDERER**
He's almost a mile from the palace; but he usually does that,
as do all men; they walk from there
to the palace gate.

**SECOND MURDERER**
A light—I see a light!                                              20

*Enter* BANQUO *and* FLEANCE, *with a torch.*

**THIRD MURDERER**
     'Tis he.

**FIRST MURDERER**
        Stand to 't.

**BANQUO**
 It will be rain tonight.

**FIRST MURDERER**
         Let it come down.

  [*They set upon* BANQUO.]


**BANQUO**
25  O, treachery! Fly, good Fleance, fly, fly, fly!

   [*Exit* FLEANCE.]

 Thou mayst revenge. [*to* MURDERER] O slave!

   [*Dies.*]


**THIRD MURDERER**
 Who did strike out the light?

**FIRST MURDERER**
         Was 't not the way?

**THIRD MURDERER**
 There's but one down; the son is fled.

**SECOND MURDERER**
30  We have lost best half of our affair.


**FIRST MURDERER**
 Well, let's away, and say how much is done.

  *Exeunt.*

BANQUO *and* FLEANCE *enter;* FLEANCE *with a torch.*

**THIRD MURDERER**
It's Banquo.

**FIRST MURDERER**
Get ready.

**BANQUO** (*to* FLEANCE)
There will be rain tonight.

**FIRST MURDERER**
Let it rain down blood.

> *The first* MURDERER *puts out the torch; the others attack* BANQUO.

**BANQUO**
Oh, treachery! Flee, good Fleance—flee, flee, flee!          25

> FLEANCE *exits running.*

(*shouting to* FLEANCE) You must seek revenge! (*to* MURDERER) Oh, villain!

> *He dies.*

**THIRD MURDERER**
Who put out the light?

**FIRST MURDERER**
Wasn't it the right thing to do?

**THIRD MURDERER**
Only one of them has been killed. The son has fled.

**SECOND MURDERER**
We have failed in the most important half of our work.          30

**FIRST MURDERER**
Well, let's go, and tell him how much we've done.

> MURDERERS *exit.*

# ACT III, SCENE IV

*[The castle.]* *Banquet prepared. Enter* MACBETH, LADY [MACBETH], ROSS, LENNOX, LORDS, *and* ATTENDANTS.

**MACBETH**
You know your own degrees; sit down.
At first and last, the hearty welcome.

**LORDS**
Thanks to your majesty.

**MACBETH**
Ourself will mingle with society
5 And play the humble host.
Our hostess keeps her state, but in best time
We will require her welcome.

**LADY MACBETH**
Pronounce it for me, sir, to all our friends,
For my heart speaks they are welcome.

*Enter* FIRST MURDERER.

**MACBETH**
10 See, they encounter thee with their hearts' thanks.
Both sides are even. Here I'll sit i' th' midst.
Be large in mirth; anon we'll drink a measure
The table round. *[Goes to* FIRST MURDERER.*]* There's
blood upon thy face.

**FIRST MURDERER**
15 'Tis Banquo's then.

**MACBETH**
'Tis better thee without than he within.
Is he dispatch'd?

**FIRST MURDERER**
My lord, his throat is cut; that I did for him.

**MACBETH**
Thou art the best o' th' cutthroats.
20 Yet he's good that did the like for Fleance;
If thou didst it, thou art the nonpareil.

# ACT 3, SCENE 4

*A formal room in the palace. A banquet is prepared.* MACBETH, LADY MACBETH, ROSS, LENNOX, LORDS, *and* SERVANTS *enter.*

**MACBETH**
You know your own ranks; sit down accordingly. From beginning to end, a hearty welcome to all.

**LORDS**
Thank you, your Majesty.

**MACBETH**
I will mingle among you
and play the humble host.                                                                              5
Our hostess stays on her throne, but when it is appropriate,
I will ask her to welcome you.

**LADY MACBETH**
Say it for me, sir, to all my friends;
for my heart says that they are welcome.

*First* MURDERER *appears at the door.*

**MACBETH**
See, they thank you from their hearts in reply.                                      10
Both sides of the table are equally full of guests. I'll sit right here, at the head.
Enjoy yourselves thoroughly. Soon we'll drink a toast
all around the table. (*to* FIRST MURDERER) There's blood on your face.

**FIRST MURDERER**
It's Banquo's, then.                                                                                        15

**MACBETH**
It's better outside you than inside him.
Is he finished off?

**FIRST MURDERER**
My lord, his throat has been cut. I did that for him.

**MACBETH**
You are the best of the cutthroats! Yet whoever killed Fleance is a good man too.                                                                                             20
If you did that, you are without equal.

**FIRST MURDERER**
  Most royal sir, Fleance is 'scaped.

**MACBETH** [*aside*]
  Then comes my fit again. I had else been perfect,
  Whole as the marble, founded as the rock,
25  As broad and general as the casing air.
  But now I am cabin'd, cribb'd, confined, bound in
  To saucy doubts and fears.—But Banquo's safe?

**FIRST MURDERER**
  Ay, my good lord: safe in a ditch he bides,
  With twenty trenched gashes on his head,
30  The least a death to nature.

**MACBETH**
                              Thanks for that.
  [*aside*] There the grown serpent lies; the worm that's fled
  Hath nature that in time will venom breed,
  No teeth for th' present.—Get thee gone. Tomorrow
35  We'll hear ourselves again.

            *Exit* FIRST MURDERER.

**LADY MACBETH**
                        My royal lord,
  You do not give the cheer. The feast is sold
  That is not often vouch'd, while 'tis a-making,
  'Tis given with welcome. To feed were best at home;
40  From thence, the sauce to meat is ceremony;
  Meeting were bare without it.

            *Enter the* GHOST OF BANQUO, *and sits in Macbeth's*
            *place.*

**MACBETH**
                              Sweet remembrancer!
  Now, good digestion wait on appetite,
  And health on both!

**LENNOX**
45                        May 't please your Highness sit.

**FIRST MURDERER**

Most royal sir, Fleance has escaped.

**MACBETH** *(aside)*

Then my fit of terror comes over me again. Otherwise, I'd have
    been completely secure—
solid as marble, steady as a rock,
as wide and free as the surrounding air.                                    25
But now I am jailed, penned, confined, locked in
with bold doubts and fears. (*to* FIRST MURDERER) But Banquo's
    safely dead?

**FIRST MURDERER**

Yes, my good lord. Safe in a ditch he remains,
with twenty trench-like gashes on his head,
the smallest of them enough to kill a man.                                   30

**MACBETH**

Thanks for doing that.
(*aside*) The grown serpent lies there. The small serpent that has
    fled
will develop venom naturally with time,
though it doesn't yet have teeth. (*to* FIRST MURDERER) Go away.
Tomorrow we'll speak together again.                                         35
        FIRST MURDERER *exits.*

**LADY MACBETH**

My royal lord,
you show no hospitality. Guests feel like they're buying their meal
if they aren't assured that it's given with welcome
while the feast is going on. Mere eating is best done at home;
outside the home, food must be flavored with ceremony;                       40
gathering for a feast is pointless without it.

        The GHOST OF BANQUO *enters and sits in Macbeth's place.*

**MACBETH**

A sweet reminder!—
(*to his* GUESTS) Now, may good digestion follow your hearty
    appetites,
and good health follow both!

**LENNOX**

Would it please your Highness to sit?                                        45

**MACBETH**

Here had we now our country's honour roofed,
Were the graced person of our Banquo present,
Who may I rather challenge for unkindness
Than pity for mischance!

**ROSS**

His absence, sir,
Lays blame upon his promise. Please 't your Highness
To grace us with your royal company.

**MACBETH**

The table's full.

**LENNOX**

Here is a place reserved, sir.

**MACBETH**

Where?

**LENNOX**

Here, my good lord. What is 't that moves your Highness?

**MACBETH**

Which of you have done this?

**LORDS**

What, my good lord?

**MACBETH** [*to the* GHOST]

Thou canst not say I did it. Never shake
Thy gory locks at me.

**ROSS**

Gentlemen, rise: his Highness is not well.

**LADY MACBETH**

Sit, worthy friends. My lord is often thus,
And hath been from his youth. Pray you, keep seat.
The fit is momentary; upon a thought
He will again be well. If much you note him,
You shall offend him and extend his passion.
Feed, and regard him not.—Are you a man?

**MACBETH**

> Here we'd have all our country's nobles under one roof,
> if only the honored Banquo were present.
> I hope to scold him for his unkindness
> rather than grieve that he's suffered some accident.

**ROSS**

> His absence, sir,  50
> proves his promise false. Would it please your Highness
> to honor us with your royal company?

**MACBETH**

> The table's full.

**LENNOX**

> A place is reserved right here, sir.

**MACBETH**

> Where?  55

**LENNOX**

> Here, my good lord. What is it that troubles your Highness?

**MACBETH**

> Which of you has done this?

**LORDS**

> What, my good lord?

**MACBETH** (*to* GHOST)

> You cannot say I did it. Don't shake
> your bloody locks of hair at me.  60

**ROSS**

> Gentlemen, rise. His Highness is not well.

**LADY MACBETH**

> Sit, worthy friends. My lord is often like this,
> and has been since he was young. Please—stay seated;
> the fit will only be momentary; he will be well again
> as quick as a thought. If you stare at him,  65
> you will offend him and make his fit last longer.
> Eat, and pay no attention to him. (*drawing* MACBETH *aside*) Are
>> you a man?

**MACBETH**

Ay, and a bold one, that dare look on that
Which might appall the devil.

**LADY MACBETH**

70                                    O proper stuff!
This is the very painting of your fear.
This is the air-drawn dagger which, you said,
Led you to Duncan. O, these flaws and starts,
Impostors to true fear, would well become
75 A woman's story at a winter's fire,
Authorized by her grandam. Shame itself!
Why do you make such faces? When all's done,
You look but on a stool.

**MACBETH**

Prithee, see there! Behold! Look! [*to the* GHOST] Lo!
80      How say you?
Why, what care I? If thou canst nod, speak too.
If charnel-houses* and our graves must send
Those that we bury back, our monuments
Shall be the maws of kites.

                 *Exit* GHOST OF BANQUO.

**LADY MACBETH**

85 What, quite unmanned in folly?

**MACBETH**

If I stand here, I saw him.

**LADY MACBETH**

                         Fie, for shame!

**MACBETH**

Blood hath been shed ere now, i' th' olden time,
Ere human statute **purged** the gentle weal;
90 Ay, and since too, murders have been perform'd
Too terrible for the ear. The time has been
That, when the brains were out, the man would die,

---

82  *charnel-houses* houses or vaults, usually associated with a church, where dead
bodies or the bones of the dead were deposited or piled up. Sometimes, because
of lack of space, bones were taken from the graveyard and put in a charnel
house.

**MACBETH**

Yes, and a bold one, since I dare look at something
which might terrify the devil.

**LADY MACBETH**

Oh, what nonsense! 70
This is just some image of what you fear—
like that imaginary dagger which you said
led you to Duncan. Oh, such sudden outbursts—
which only appear to be fearful—would be better suited
to a woman's story by a winter's fire, 75
sworn to by her grandmother. For shame!
Why do you make such faces? When all's said and done,
you're only looking at a stool.

**MACBETH**

Please, see it! Observe, look! (*to the* GHOST) Oh! What do
you want to say? 80
Why, what do I care? You can nod, so speak, too.
If charnel houses and our graves send
back to us the dead that we bury, our real tombs
will be in the stomachs of birds.

GHOST OF BANQUO *vanishes.*

**LADY MACBETH**

What's this—has foolishness stolen your manhood? 85

**MACBETH**

As sure as I stand here, I saw him.

**LADY MACBETH**

Ugh, for shame!

**MACBETH**

Blood has been shed before now, in olden times,
before humane laws made the nation more civilized;
yes, and even since then, murders have been committed, 90
too terrible to hear of. There was a time
when, once his brains were knocked out, a man would die,

And there an end; but now they rise again,
With twenty mortal murders on their crowns,
95 And push us from our stools. This is more strange
Than such a murder is.

**LADY MACBETH**
                      My worthy lord,
Your noble friends do lack you.

**MACBETH**
                            I do forget.
100 Do not muse at me, my most worthy friends,
I have a strange **infirmity**, which is nothing
To those that know me. Come, love and health to all.
Then I'll sit down.—Give me some wine; fill full.

*Enter* GHOST OF BANQUO.

I drink to the general joy o' th' whole table,
105 And to our dear friend Banquo, whom we miss.
Would he were here! To all and him we thirst,
And all to all.

**LORDS**
                Our duties, and the pledge.

**MACBETH**
Avaunt! And quit my sight! Let the earth hide thee!
110 Thy bones are marrowless, thy blood is cold;
Thou hast no speculation in those eyes
Which thou dost glare with!

**LADY MACBETH**
                          Think of this, good peers,
But as a thing of custom, 'tis no other.
115 Only it spoils the pleasure of the time.

**MACBETH**
What man dare, I dare.
Approach thou like the rugged Russian bear,
The armed rhinoceros, or the Hyrcan\* tiger;

---

118  *Hyrcan* from Hyrcania, an ancient region south of the Caspian Sea and reported
by Pliny to be a place where tigers were bred

and that would be the end of it. But now the dead rise again,
with twenty deadly wounds on their heads,
and push us off our stools. This is stranger                    95
than such a murder itself.

**LADY MACBETH**
My worthy lord,
Your noble friends miss you at the table.

**MACBETH**
I had forgotten them.
(*to* GUESTS) Don't be amazed at me, my most worthy friends.    100
I have a strange illness, which means nothing
to those who know me. Come, let's drink to everyone's love and
    health.
Then I'll sit down.— Give me some wine. Fill it full.

> GHOST OF BANQUO *enters.*

I drink to the general joy of everyone at the table—
and to our dear friend Banquo, whom we miss.                    105
If only he were here! I want to drink to him and to everyone,
and let all drink to all.

**LORDS**
We drink to our allegiance, and to your toast.

**MACBETH**
> (*seeing* GHOST OF BANQUO)

Go away, and get out my sight! Hide yourself in the earth!
Your bones have no marrow; your blood is cold;                  110
You have no vision in those eyes
from which you glare.

**LADY MACBETH** (*to* GUESTS)
Good nobles, think of this
as just a habit of his; that's all it is;
it only spoils the pleasure of the occasion.                    115

**MACBETH** (*to* GHOST)
What any man dares, I dare.
So approach me looking like a rugged Russian bear,
an armored rhinoceros, or a tiger of Hyrcania;

Take any shape but that, and my firm nerves
120 Shall never tremble. Or be alive again,
And dare me to the desert with thy sword.
If trembling I inhabit then, protest me
The baby of a girl. Hence, horrible shadow!
Unreal mock'ry, hence!

*Exit* GHOST OF BANQUO.

125 Why, so: being gone,
I am a man again.—Pray you, sit still.

**LADY MACBETH**
You have displaced the **mirth**, broke the good meeting,
With most admired disorder.

**MACBETH**
                                    Can such things be,
130 And overcome us like a summer's cloud,
Without our special wonder? You make me strange
Even to the **disposition** that I owe,
When now I think you can behold such sights,
And keep the natural ruby of your cheeks,
135 When mine is **blanched** with fear.

**ROSS**
                                    What sights, my lord?

**LADY MACBETH**
I pray you, speak not; he grows worse and worse;
Question enrages him. At once, good night:
Stand not upon the order of your going,
140 But go at once.

**LENNOX**
                        Good night, and better health
Attend his Majesty!

**LADY MACBETH**
                        A kind good night to all!

[*Exeunt* LORDS.]

take any shape but this, and my firm muscles
will never tremble. Or come to life again                                    120
and dare me to fight with swords in some lonely place.
If I continue to tremble then, call me
a baby girl. Away, you horrible shadow!
You unreal mockery, away!

        *GHOST OF BANQUO exits.*

Why, now that it's gone,                                                     125
I am a man again. (*to* GUESTS) Please, everyone, sit still.

**LADY MACBETH** (*to* MACBETH)
You have chased away our happiness, and spoiled this good
    gathering
with a most amazing outburst.

**MACBETH**
Can such things happen,
and pass over us like a summer's cloud,                                      130
without our taking special notice? You make me wonder
what kind of person I am,
now that I see how you can look on such sights
and keep the natural rosiness of your cheeks,
when mine are pale with fear.                                                135

**ROSS**
What sights, my lord?

**LADY MACBETH**
I beg you, don't speak. He grows worse and worse.
Questions will enrage him. Quickly—let's say good night.
Don't worry about leaving in the order of your ranks,
just go at once.                                                             140

**LENNOX**
Good night—and may his Majesty
soon feel better.

**LADY MACBETH**
A kind good night to all.

        *LORDS exit.*

**MACBETH**

It will have blood, they say: blood will have blood.
145  Stones have been known to move and trees to speak;
Augurs and understood relations have
By maggot-pies and choughs and rooks brought forth
The secret'st man of blood. What is the night?

**LADY MACBETH**

Almost at odds with morning, which is which.

**MACBETH**

150  How say'st thou, that Macduff denies his person
At our great bidding?

**LADY MACBETH**

                    Did you send to him, sir?

**MACBETH**

I hear it by the way; but I will send.
There's not a one of them but in his house
155  I keep a servant fee'd. I will tomorrow,
And betimes I will, to the Weïrd Sisters:
More shall they speak, for now I am bent to know
By the worst means, the worst. For mine own good
All causes shall give way. I am in blood
160  Stepped in so far that, should I wade no more,
Returning were as tedious as go o'er.
Strange things I have in head, that will to hand,
Which must be acted ere they may be scanned.

**LADY MACBETH**

You lack the season of all natures, sleep.

**MACBETH**

165  Come, we'll to sleep. My strange and self-abuse
Is the initiate fear that wants hard use.
We are yet but young in deed.

        *Exeunt.*

**MACBETH**

The murdered will have revenge, they say; bloodshed requires
more bloodshed.
Stones have been known to move and trees to speak;     145
and well-understood messages
told by magpies, jackdaws, and crows have revealed
the best-hidden murderer.—What time of night is it?

**LADY MACBETH**

So near morning, it's hard to say whether it's morning or night.

**MACBETH**

What do you think of the fact that Macduff refused to come to
the feast     150
at our command?

**LADY MACBETH**

Did you send for him, sir?

**MACBETH**

I heard talk of his absence, but I will send for more information.
In each of the nobles' houses,
I keep a paid spy. I'll go tomorrow—     155
and very early—to visit the Witches.
They'll tell me more, for now I am determined to learn
the worst news from the worst sources. For my own good,
everything else must take second place. I have waded so deep
in blood that, even if I tried to stop,     160
it would be as hard to go back as to wade the rest of the way
across.
I've got strange things in mind that must be carried out—
and they must be done without taking time to think about them.

**LADY MACBETH**

You lack the preservative of all living creatures, sleep.

**MACBETH**

Come, we'll go to sleep. My strange delusion     165
is the fear of a beginner who needs to be toughened by
experience.
We are still only novices in evil.

    *They exit.*

# ACT III, SCENE V

[*A Witches' haunt.*] *Thunder. Enter the three* WITCHES, *meeting* HECATE.

**FIRST WITCH**
Why, how now, Hecate! You look angerly.

**HECATE**
Have I not reason, beldams as you are,
Saucy and overbold? How did you dare
To trade and traffic with Macbeth
5   In riddles and affairs of death;
And I, the mistress of your charms,
The close contriver of all harms,
Was never call'd to bear my part,
Or show the glory of our art?
10   And, which is worse, all you have done
Hath been but for a wayward son,
Spiteful and wrathful, who, as others do,
Loves for his own ends, not for you.
But make amends now: get you gone,
15   And at the pit of Acheron*
Meet me i' th' morning. Thither he
Will come to know his destiny.
Your vessels and your spells provide,
Your charms and everything beside.
20   I am for th' air; this night I'll spend
Unto a dismal and a fatal end.
Great business must be wrought ere noon.
Upon the corner of the moon
There hangs a vap'rous drop profound;
25   I'll catch it ere it come to ground.
And that distill'd by magic sleights
Shall raise such artificial sprites
As by the strength of their illusion
Shall draw him on to his confusion.
30   He shall spurn fate, scorn death, and bear

---

15   *pit of Acheron*   Perhaps this refers to the Scottish cavern where the Witches
assemble in Act IV, Scene i. Acheron is the name of a river in Hades.

# ACT 3, SCENE 5

*A heath. Thunder. The three* WITCHES *enter, meeting* HECATE.

**FIRST WITCH**

Why, what is it, Hecate? You look angry.

**HECATE**

Haven't I got reason to be since you hags are so
impudent and overly bold? How dare you
deal with Macbeth
in the riddles and business of death—                                    5
while I, the teacher of your spells
and the secret inventor of all evils,
was never called to play my part,
or to show the glory of our art?
What's worse, all you have done                                          10
has only been for a headstrong,
spiteful, and wrathful follower—who, as others do,
cares for his own purposes, not yours.
But make amends now. Leave here at once
and meet me in the morning
at the pit of Acheron. He will come                                      15
there to learn his destiny.
Bring along your tools, spells
charms, and everything else that's needed.
I'll take to the air. I'll spend tonight                                 20
arranging a disastrous and deadly conclusion.
Great business must be done before noon.
Upon the corner of the moon,
there hangs a heavy drop of moisture.
I'll catch it before it hits the ground;                                 25
when it's been distilled by my magic,
it will raise up such unnatural spirits of witchcraft
that by the strength of their deceptions,
they will lead him on to greater confusion.
He will reject fate, mock death, and value                               30

He hopes 'bove wisdom, grace, and fear.
And you all know, security
Is mortals' chiefest enemy.

*Music and song.*

Hark! I am called; my little spirit, see,
35 Sits in a foggy cloud and stays for me.

*Exit.*

**FIRST WITCH**
Come, let's make haste. She'll soon be back again.

*Exeunt.*

his hopes more than he does wisdom, virtue, and fear.
And you all know that over-confidence
is mortals' greatest enemy.

*Music and a song is heard offstage.*

Listen! I'm being called. See, how my little spirit
sits in a foggy cloud and waits for me.                    35

    HECATE *exits.*

**FIRST WITCH**
Come, let's hurry. She'll soon be back again.

    *They exit.*

# ACT III, SCENE VI

*[The palace.]* Enter LENNOX *and another* LORD.

**LENNOX**
    My former speeches have but hit your thoughts,
    Which can interpret farther. Only I say
    Things have been strangely borne. The gracious Duncan
    Was pitied of Macbeth; marry, he was dead.
5    And the right-valiant Banquo walked too late;
    Whom, you may say, if 't please you, Fleance killed,
    For Fleance fled. Men must not walk too late.
    Who cannot want the thought, how monstrous
    It was for Malcolm and for Donalbain
10    To kill their gracious father? Damned fact!
    How it did grieve Macbeth! Did he not straight
    In pious rage, the two delinquents tear,
    That were the slaves of drink and thralls of sleep?
    Was not that nobly done? Ay, and wisely too;
15    For 'twould have angered any heart alive
    To hear the men deny 't. So that I say
    He has borne all things well. And I do think
    That had he Duncan's sons under his key—
    As, an 't please heaven, he shall not—they should find
20    What 'twere to kill a father. So should Fleance.
    But, peace! For from broad words and 'cause he failed
    His presence at the tyrant's feast, I hear,
    Macduff lives in disgrace. Sir, can you tell
    Where he bestows himself?

**LORD**
25                        The son of Duncan,
    From whom this tyrant holds the due of birth,
    Lives in the English court and is received
    Of the most pious Edward* with such grace
    That the **malevolence** of fortune nothing
30    Takes from his high respect. Thither Macduff
    Is gone to pray the holy King upon his aid

---

28   *Edward* Edward the Confessor, King of England 1042–66

# ACT 3, SCENE 6

*Forres. The palace.* LENNOX *and another* LORD *enter.*

**LENNOX** (*ironically*)
What I've been saying, you've been thinking, too—
so draw your own conclusions. I only say
that things have been managed strangely. Macbeth pitied
the kindly Duncan; and indeed, he was murdered.
And the most valiant Banquo walked outside too late—     5
and you may say, if you wish, that Fleance killed him,
for Fleance fled. Men must not walk outside too late.
Who can help but think how monstrous
it was for Malcolm and Donalbain
to kill their kindly father? Damned evil deed!     10
How it grieved Macbeth! And right away,
in religious rage, didn't he kill the two wrongdoers
while they were slaves of drink and captives of sleep?
Wasn't that nobly done? Yes, and wisely, too,
for it would have angered any heart alive     15
to hear the men deny it. And that's why I say
he has managed all things well. And I think,
if Macbeth had Duncan's sons under lock and key—
may it please heaven that he never does!—they'd learn
what it means to kill a father. So would Fleance.     20
But let's be quiet. For because of his bold words, and because
        he failed
to attend the tyrant's feast, I hear
Macduff lives in disgrace. Sir, can you tell me
where he's keeping himself?

**LORD**
Malcolm, the son of King Duncan,     25
from whom this tyrant has stolen his birthright,
lives in the English court and is treated
by the most religious King Edward with such kindness,
that fortune's cruelty cannot lessen
the high respect in which he is held. Macduff has gone there     30
to ask the holy King, on Malcolm's behalf,

To wake Northumberland and warlike Siward,*
That, by the help of these, with Him above
To ratify the work, we may again
35    Give to our tables meat, sleep to our nights,
Free from our feasts and banquets bloody knives,
Do faithful homage and receive free honours:
All which we pine for now. And this report
Hath so exasperate the king that he
40    Prepares for some attempt of war.

**LENNOX**

                              Sent he to Macduff?

**LORD**

He did, and with an absolute "Sir, not I,"
The cloudy messenger turns me his back
And hums, as who should say "You'll rue the time
45    That clogs me with this answer."

**LENNOX**

                                    And that well might
Advise him to a caution, t' hold what distance
His wisdom can provide. Some holy angel
Fly to the court of England and unfold
50    His message ere he come, that a swift blessing
May soon return to this our suffering country
Under a hand accursed!

**LORD**

                          I'll send my prayers with him.

        *Exeunt.*

---

32    *Siward* Earl of Northumberland

to stir up Northumberland and the warlike Siward
so that with their help—and also with the support
of God above for their cause—we may again
have food on our tables and sleep during our nights;                    35
free our feasts and banquets from bloody knives;
receive freely granted honors in return for nothing more than our
    faithful devotion;
all of which we yearn for now. News of this
has so exasperated Macbeth that he
is preparing for war.                                                   40

**LENNOX**

Did he send for Macduff?

**LORD**

He did—and when Macduff flatly replied, "Sir, I'll not come,"
the sullen messenger turned his back
and hummed, as if to say, "You'll regret the moment
when you burdened me with this answer."                                 45

**LENNOX**

That might well
teach Macduff to be cautious, and to use his wisdom
to keep as much distance as possible from Macbeth. May some
    holy angel
fly to the court of England and deliver
Macduff's message before he gets there, so that a swift
    blessing                                                              50
may soon return to our country, which suffers
under a cursed hand!

**LORD**

I'll send my prayers with him.

    *They exit.*

# Act III Review

## Discussion Questions

1. What is the importance of Fleance's escape?

2. What does Macbeth mean when he says "blood will have blood" on page 146?

3. From the point of view of one of their servants, describe how Macbeth and Lady Macbeth's behaviors have changed since they have become King and Queen.

4. What does Macbeth's attitude toward Macduff show about his state of mind?

5. Do you think Scene vi is important to the play? Explain why or why not.

6. What kind of a ruler has Macbeth become by the end of Act III? Find evidence from the play to support your answer.

## Literary Elements

1. Review Hecate's speech on pages 148–150 and compare its **verse structure** to other speeches in the play. Why do you think critics are so sure that someone other than Shakespeare wrote this speech?

2. In the banquet scene, Macbeth believes that he can see the ghost of Banquo. Yet, no one else present at the feast sees the apparition. What is the possible **implication**?

3. Shakespeare often made **allusions** to figures and stories from ancient Greece and Rome in his writing. In Act III, Scene i, Macbeth says, "My genius is rebuked, as it is said / Mark Antony's was by Caesar." Who is Caesar, and what do you think this reference suggests? Find another allusion in *Macbeth* and explain its meaning and how it adds to the play.

# Writing Prompts

1. Pretend you attended the coronation ceremony of Macbeth at Scone. Write a diary entry describing the ceremony and the events that occurred. Use the language of Shakespeare in writing the diary entry.

2. From the point of view of one of Macbeth's spies in the castle of another Scottish thane, write an account of any activities in the household that you think Macbeth would want to know about. Use the language of Shakespeare in writing the report to Macbeth.

3. Shakespeare often gave "dying speeches" to characters in his plays, but he does not do so for Duncan or Banquo. Write a dying speech for either of these characters, imparting information they might like others to know as well as expressing emotions they might feel on their deathbeds.

4. From what you know about Lady Macbeth so far, make a list of her character traits. Then, list the proof from the text that supports each trait. Finally, write a description of Lady Macbeth based on the first three acts. Use a graphic organizer like the one below to organize your thoughts.

| Character Traits | | Proof |
|---|---|---|
| 1. *anxious* | ➡ | *"Nought's had, all's spent, / Where our desire is got without content."* (Act III, Scene ii) |
| 2. | ➡ | |

# Macbeth

## ACT IV

*The Three Witches*, Alexandre-Marie Colin, 1827

"By the pricking of my
thumbs, something
wicked this way comes."

# Before You Read

1.  Do you think deeds such as murder will *inevitably* be punished? Explain.

2.  What does Macbeth's future hold? Give reasons for your answer.

3.  Consider whether the slaughter in Act IV, Scene ii is necessary.

# Literary Elements

1.  A **symbol** is a person, object, action, or place that stands for something beyond its obvious meaning. In Macbeth, Act II, Scene i, Macbeth thinks he sees a dagger floating in the air before him. The dagger probably symbolizes the "bloody business" that he must carry out—killing Duncan—if he is to become king.

2.  The **mood** is the overall feeling or atmosphere an author creates with his or her selection of details. *Macbeth* opens on a barren heath with three Witches muttering incantations over the background sounds of thunder and lightning. The mood is dark and foreboding.

3.  **Hyperbole** is exaggeration that you are not supposed to take literally. In Act III, Scene iv, Macbeth says, "I am in blood / Stepp'd in so far that, should I wade no more, / Returning were as tedious as go o'er." He is claiming that it is just as easy to go forward with his bloody plans as to go backward, which is not necessarily true.

4.  **Foreshadowing** refers to hints about what might happen at a later point in the plot. In Act III, Scene ii, Macbeth says to his wife, "We have scorch'd the snake, not kill'd it." In other words, they have not put trouble to rest by killing Duncan.

# Words to Know

The following vocabulary words appear in Act IV in the original text of Shakespeare's play. However, they are words that are still commonly used. Read the definitions here and pay attention to the words as you read the play (they will be in boldfaced type).

| | |
|---|---|
| **abjure** | disregard; renounce |
| **appease** | calm; soothe |
| **avaricious** | greedy; acquisitive |
| **credulous** [over-credulous] | naive; gullible |
| **desolate** | lonely; abandoned |
| **detraction** | backbiting; belittling |
| **diminutive** | tiny; miniature |
| **impediments** | obstacles; obstructions |
| **interdiction** | ban; taboo |
| **judicious** | thoughtful; sage |
| **laudable** | praiseworthy; commendable |
| **reconciled** | made friends; brought together |
| **redress** | make up for; atone |
| **voluptuousness** | desire for pleasure or indulgence |

# Act Summary

The Witches decide to trick Macbeth into thinking he is secure. They warn Macbeth to beware of Macduff, the Thane of Fife. But they also assure Macbeth that no man born of a woman can kill him. Macbeth gloats with joy.

The Witches then tell Macbeth that he will never be defeated in battle until Birnam Wood moves toward his castle Dunsinane. Macbeth is even more delighted. A moving forest? Impossible!

But Macbeth realizes that the Witches' third prediction will prove true: Banquo's offspring will someday rule Scotland.

After meeting the Witches, Macbeth hears that Macduff, the Thane of Fife, has gone to England, unwisely leaving his wife and children behind.

Robert Taber as Macduff, Lyceum Theatre, London, 1898

Enraged, Macbeth sends murderers to Macduff's castle to slaughter Macduff's entire family.

Not knowing of this horrible deed, Macduff arrives in England and meets with the exiled Malcolm. He describes how Scotland is on the verge of rebellion. He urges Malcolm to invade Scotland, depose Macbeth, and become King.

At first, Malcolm doesn't trust Macduff. He suspects that Macduff is really on Macbeth's side. But after testing Macduff's loyalty, Malcolm tells him that an English army is ready to march against Macbeth.

At that very moment, Ross, another thane, arrives to tell Macduff of his family's terrible fate. Sorrowful and enraged, Macduff vows vengeance against Macbeth.

# ACT IV, SCENE I

*[A Witches' haunt.]* *Thunder. Enter the three* WITCHES.

**FIRST WITCH**
Thrice the brinded cat hath mewed.

**SECOND WITCH**
Thrice and once the hedge-pig whined.

**THIRD WITCH**
Harpier* cries, "'tis time, 'tis time!"

**FIRST WITCH**
Round about the cauldron go;
5   In the poisoned entrails throw.
Toad, that under cold stone
Days and nights has thirty-one
Sweltered venom sleeping got,
Boil thou first i' th' charmed pot.

**ALL**
10  Double, double toil and trouble;
Fire burn and cauldron bubble.

**SECOND WITCH**
Fillet of a fenny snake,
In the cauldron boil and bake;
Eye of newt and toe of frog,
15  Wool of bat and tongue of dog,
Adder's fork and blindworm's* sting,
Lizard's leg and howlet's wing,
For a charm of pow'rful trouble,
Like a hell-broth boil and bubble.

**ALL**
20  Double, double toil and trouble;
Fire burn and cauldron bubble.

**THIRD WITCH**
Scale of dragon, tooth of wolf,

---

3   *Harpier*  the "familiar" of the Third Witch
16  *blindworm*  a harmless kind of legless lizard thought poisonous by Elizabethans

# ACT 4, SCENE 1

*A dark cave. Thunder.* WITCHES *enter.*

**FIRST WITCH**
> The streaked cat has mewed three times.

**SECOND WITCH**
> The hedgehog has whined three times, plus one.

**THIRD WITCH**
> Harpier cries, "It's time, it's time!"

**FIRST WITCH**
> Go all around the cauldron;
> throw in the poisoned guts.
> Here's a toad that has sweated out venom
> while sleeping for thirty-one days and nights
> under a cold stone;
> boil it first in the magical pot.

5

**ALL**
> Let toil and trouble grow double everywhere;
> let the fire burn and the cauldron bubble.

10

**SECOND WITCH**
> Boil and bake in the cauldron
> a slice of a snake from the swamp,
> the eye of a newt and the toe of a frog,
> the wool of a bat and the tongue of a dog,
> an adder's forked tongue and a slow-worm's sting,
> a lizard's leg and a young owl's wing,
> to cast a spell for powerful trouble,
> boil and bubble like a hell-broth.

15

**ALL**
> Let toil and trouble grow double everywhere;
> let the fire burn and the cauldron bubble.

20

**THIRD WITCH**
> The scale of a dragon, the tooth of a wolf,

Witches' mummy, maw and gulf
Of the ravined salt-sea shark,
25    Root of hemlock digged i' th' dark,
Liver of blaspheming Jew,
Gall of goat, and slips of yew
Silvered in the moon's eclipse,
Nose of Turk and Tartar's lips,
30    Finger of birth-strangled babe
Ditch-delivered by a drab,
Make the gruel thick and slab.
Add thereto a tiger's chaudron,
For th' ingredients of our cauldron.

**ALL**

35    Double, double toil and trouble;
Fire burn and cauldron bubble.

**SECOND WITCH**

Cool it with a baboon's blood,
Then the charm is firm and good.

*Enter* HECATE *to the other three* WITCHES.

**HECATE**

O, well done! I commend your pains;
40    And every one shall share i' th' gains.
And now about the cauldron sing,
Like elves and fairies in a ring,
Enchanting all that you put in.

*Music and a song: "Black spirits," etc.* *

[ *Exit* HECTATE. ]

**SECOND WITCH**

By the pricking of my thumbs,
45    Something wicked this way comes:
[*knocking*] Open, locks,
Whoever knocks!

*Enter* MACBETH.

---

43   *Black Spirits*   The text of a song beginning in this way appears in Thomas
Middleton's "The Witch," but there it is sung by the son of Hecate. Actually this
song is irrelevant to Shakespeare's play and may have been added for
entertainment.

the mummified flesh of a witch, the stomach and throat
of a salt-sea shark glutted with prey,
the root of a hemlock plant, dug up in the dark,                    25
the liver of a blasphemous Jew,
the bile of a goat and seedlings of a yew tree
cut off during an eclipse of the moon,
the nose of a Turk and a Tartar's lips,
the finger of a baby strangled at birth                            30
after being born in a ditch to a prostitute.
Make the gruel thick and slimy.
Add to the mix a tiger's guts
for the ingredients of our cauldron.

**ALL**

Let toil and trouble grow double everywhere;                       35
let the fire burn and the cauldron bubble.

**SECOND WITCH**

Cool it with a baboon's blood.
Now the spell is thick and ready.

> HECATE *enters.*

**HECATE**

Oh, well done! I praise your efforts,
and every one of you will share in the profits.                    40
And now, sing around the cauldron
like elves and fairies in a ring,
bewitching all that you've put in.

> *Music and a song.*

> HECATE *exits.*

**SECOND WITCH**

I can tell by a tingling in my thumbs
that something wicked is coming this way.                          45

> (*knocking*)

Locks, open yourselves
to whomever knocks.

> MACBETH *enters.*

**MACBETH**
How now, you secret, black, and midnight hags!
What is 't you do?

**ALL**
50                               A deed without a name.

**MACBETH**
I conjure you, by that which you profess,
Howe'er you come to know it, answer me:
Though you untie the winds and let them fight
Against the churches; though the yeasty waves
55    Confound and swallow navigation up;
Though bladed corn be lodged and trees blown down;
Though castles topple on their warders' heads;
Though palaces and pyramids do slope
Their heads to their foundations; though the treasure
60    Of nature's germens* tumble all together,
Even till destruction sicken; answer me
To what I ask you.

**FIRST WITCH**
Speak.

**SECOND WITCH**
Demand.

**THIRD WITCH**
65                                          We'll answer.

**FIRST WITCH**
Say, if th' rather hear it from our mouths,
Or from our masters?

**MACBETH**
Call 'em, let me see 'em.

**FIRST WITCH**
Pour in sow's blood, that hath eaten
70    Her nine farrow; grease that's sweaten
From the murderer's gibbet throw
Into the flame.

---

60   *nature's germens*  the accumulated store of those elemental seeds or germs from
which everything in the future is to spring

**MACBETH**

What have we here, you mysterious, black hags of midnight!
What is it that you do?

**ALL**

A deed without a name.                                           50

**MACBETH**

I command you by the black arts that you follow—
however you came to learn them—to answer me.
Even if you unleash the winds and let them storm
against the churches; even if foamy waves
destroy and sink ships;                                          55
even if ripe wheat is flattened and trees blown down;
even if castles fall on the heads of those who live in them;
even if the tops of palaces and pyramids
are leveled to their bases; even if the precious
seeds of all uncreated things tumble together               60
until destruction itself grows sick of its work; answer
the questions I ask you.

**FIRST WITCH**

Speak.

**SECOND WITCH**

Demand.

**THIRD WITCH**

We'll answer.                                                   65

**FIRST WITCH**

Tell us if you would rather hear it from our mouths,
or the mouths of our masters.

**MACBETH**

Call them. Let me see them.

**FIRST WITCH**

Pour in the cauldron the blood of a sow that has eaten
her nine young; also throw into the flame                   70
grease that has collected
on a murderer's gallows.

**ALL**

Come, high or low,
Thyself and office deftly show!

*Thunder.* FIRST APPARITION: *An Armed Head.*

**MACBETH**

75    Tell me, thou unknown power—

**FIRST WITCH**

He knows thy thought:
Hear his speech, but say thou nought.

**FIRST APPARITION**

Macbeth! Macbeth! Macbeth! Beware Macduff!
Beware the Thane of Fife. Dismiss me. Enough.

*He descends.*

**MACBETH**

80    Whate'er thou art, for thy good caution thanks:
Thou hast harped my fear aright. But one word more—

**FIRST WITCH**

He will not be commanded. Here's another,
More potent than the first.

*Thunder.* SECOND APPARITION: *A Bloody Child.*

**SECOND APPARITION**

Macbeth! Macbeth! Macbeth!

**MACBETH**

85    Had I three ears, I'd hear thee.

**SECOND APPARITION**

Be bloody, bold, and resolute! Laugh to scorn
The power of man, for none of woman born
Shall harm Macbeth.

*Descends.*

**MACBETH**

Then live, Macduff: what need I fear of thee?
90    But yet I'll make assurance double sure,
And take a bond of fate. Thou shalt not live,
That I may tell pale-hearted fear it lies,
And sleep in spite of thunder.

**ALL**

Come, you high and low spirits;
show yourselves, and skillfully do your work!

*Thunder. The* FIRST APPARITION, *an armored* HEAD, *appears.*

**MACBETH**

Tell me, you unknown power— 75

**FIRST WITCH**

He knows your thoughts.
Listen to his speech, but don't say anything.

**FIRST APPARITION**

Macbeth! Macbeth! Macbeth! Beware of Macduff,
Beware of the Thane of Fife. Let me go. I've said enough.

*The* FIRST APPARITION *disappears.*

**MACBETH**

Whoever you are, thanks for your timely warning. 80
You have touched on my very fear. But tell me one more thing—

**FIRST WITCH**

He cannot be commanded. Here's another spirit
more powerful than the first.

*Thunder. The* SECOND APPARITION, *a bloody* CHILD, *appears.*

**SECOND APPARITION**

Macbeth! Macbeth! Macbeth!—

**MACBETH**

I'm all ears, listening to you. 85

**SECOND APPARITION**

Be ruthless, bold, and decisive. Laugh scornfully
at the power of men—for no man born to a woman
can harm Macbeth.

*The* SECOND APPARITION *disappears.*

**MACBETH**

Then live on, Macduff; why should I fear you?
But still, I'll make myself doubly confident, 90
and force fate to stand by its promise. You will not live,
so I may tell my faint-hearted fear that it lies,
and sleep even through thunder.

*Thunder.* THIRD APPARITION: *A Child Crowned, with a tree in his hand.*

What is this
95 That rises like the issue of a king,
And wears upon his baby-brow the round
And top of sovereignty?

**ALL**
Listen, but speak not to 't.

**THIRD APPARITION**
Be lion-mettled, proud, and take no care
100 Who chafes, who frets, or where conspirers are.
Macbeth shall never vanquish'd be until
Great Birnam Wood to high Dunsinane Hill
Shall come against him.

*Descends.*

**MACBETH**
That will never be
105 Who can impress the forest, bid the tree
Unfix his earth-bound root? Sweet bodements, good!
Rebellion's head, rise never till the Wood
Of Birnam rise, and our high-placed Macbeth
Shall live the lease of nature, pay his breath
110 To time and mortal custom. Yet my heart
Throbs to know one thing. Tell me, if your art
Can tell so much: shall Banquo's issue ever
Reign in this kingdom?

**ALL**
Seek to know no more.

**MACBETH**
115 I will be satisfied. Deny me this,
And an eternal curse fall on you! Let me know.
Why sinks that cauldron? And what noise is this?

*Hautboys.*

*Thunder. The* THIRD APPARITION, *a crowned* CHILD *with a tree in his hand, appears.*

What is this spirit,
who looks like a king's offspring as he rises,                    95
wearing upon his baby's brow a crown—
the highest symbol of power?

**ALL**

Listen, but do not speak to it.

**THIRD APPARITION.**

Be strong like a lion and proud, and do not worry
about anyone who angers or troubles you, or where
    conspirators might be.                                        100
Macbeth will never be defeated until
great Birnam Wood marches
to fight against him.

> *The* THIRD APPARITION *disappears.*

**MACBETH**

That will never be.
Who can draft the forest into service, command a tree             105
to pull up its earthbound roots? These are good, sweet
    prophecies!
Rebellious, slain Banquo, you'll never rise until the woods
of Birnam move; so highly placed Macbeth
will live out his normal life span, breathing serenely
for a long time, dying a natural death. Still, my throbbing heart  110
longs to know one thing. Tell me—if your skills
can tell so much—will Banquo's descendants ever
reign in this kingdom?

**ALL**

Seek to know no more.

**MACBETH**

I must learn everything. Refuse to tell me this,                  115
and let an eternal curse fall on you! Let me know!

> *The cauldron sinks through a trapdoor. Oboes are heard offstage.*

Why is the cauldron sinking? And what is this music?

**FIRST WITCH**

Show!

**SECOND WITCH**

Show!

**THIRD WITCH**

120  Show!

**ALL**

Show his eyes, and grieve his heart;
Come like shadows, so depart!

> *A show of eight kings, [the eighth king] with a glass in
> his hand, and* BANQUO *last.*

**MACBETH**

Thou art too like the spirit of Banquo. Down!
Thy crown does sear mine eyeballs. And thy hair,
125  Thou other gold-bound brow, is like the first.
A third is like the former.—Filthy hags!
Why do you show me this?—A fourth! Start, eyes!
What, will the line stretch out to th' crack of doom?
Another yet! A seventh! I'll see no more.
130  And yet the eighth appears, who bears a glass
Which shows me many more, and some I see
That twofold balls and treble scepters* carry:
Horrible sight! Now, I see, 'tis true;
For the blood-boltered Banquo smiles upon me,
135  And points at them for his. What, is this so?

**FIRST WITCH**

Ay, sir, all this is so. But why
Stands Macbeth thus amazedly?

---

132  *twofold balls and treble scepters* The balls may refer to the double coronation of
James I in Scotland and in England. The treble scepters are the two used for
investment in the English coronation, and the one used in the Scottish
coronation. The passage is a tribute to James I and the union of Great Britain
under him.

**FIRST WITCH**
Show him!

**SECOND WITCH**
Show him!

**THIRD WITCH**
Show him!                                                          120

**ALL**
Show his eyes the future, and bring his heart grief.
Come and go like shadows.

> *A parade of eight kings enters, the last with a mirror in his hand;*
> *the* GHOST OF BANQUO *follows them.*

**MACBETH**
You look too much like the spirit of Banquo. Get away!
Your crown scorches my eyeballs. And you, the next one—
the hair on your golden-crowned head is like the first.          125
The third is like the second.—Filthy hags,
why are you showing me this?—A fourth! My eyes pop out of
    their sockets!
What, will this parade of kings continue until thunder announces
    Judgment Day?
Still another? A seventh! I'll not look anymore.
And even an eighth appears, holding a mirror                      130
which shows me many more kings—and some I see
carrying double globes and triple scepters.
What a horrible sight! Now I see that it's true,
for Banquo, with his blood-matted hair, smiles at me
and claims them as his descendants.

> APPARITIONS *vanish.*

What, is this true?                                              135

**FIRST WITCH**
Yes, sir, all this is true. But why
is Macbeth standing there looking so amazed?

Come, sisters, cheer we up his sprites,
And show the best of our delights:
140      I'll charm the air to give a sound,
While you perform your antic round,
That this great King may kindly say
Our duties did his welcome pay.

*Music. The* WITCHES *dance, and vanish.*

**MACBETH**
Where are they? Gone? Let this pernicious hour
145      Stand aye accursed in the calendar!
Come in, without there!

*Enter* LENNOX.

**LENNOX**
                        What's your Grace's will?

**MACBETH**
Saw you the Weïrd Sisters?

**LENNOX**
                        No, my lord.

**MACBETH**
150      Came they not by you?

**LENNOX**
                      No, indeed, my lord.

**MACBETH**
Infected be the air whereon they ride,
And damn'd all those that trust them! I did hear
The galloping of horse. Who was 't came by?

**LENNOX**
155      'Tis two or three, my lord, that bring you word
Macduff is fled to England.

**MACBETH**
                  Fled to England?

**LENNOX**
Ay, my good lord.

**MACBETH** [*aside*]
Time, thou anticipat'st my dread exploits.

Come on, sisters, let's cheer up his spirits
and give him the best of our entertainment.
I'll cast a spell on the air to make music,                    140
while you perform a fantastic, circular dance —
so this great King may kindly say
that we paid proper homage to him.

    *Music. The* WITCHES *dance and then vanish.*

**MACBETH**
Where are they? Gone? Let this destructive hour
be recorded as cursed in the calendar!                         145
Come in, you who wait outside there.

    LENNOX *enters.*

**LENNOX**
What does your Grace want?

**MACBETH**
Did you see the Witches?

**LENNOX**
No, my lord.

**MACBETH**
Didn't they go past you?                                       150

**LENNOX**
Certainly not, my lord.

**MACBETH**
May the air they ride on be diseased,
and may all who trust them be damned! I heard
galloping horses. Who just arrived?

**LENNOX**
Two or three men, my lord, who bring you word             155
that Macduff has fled to England.

**MACBETH**
Fled to England?

**LENNOX**
Yes, my good lord.

**MACBETH** (*aside*)
Time, you foresee my dreadful undertaking.

160  The flighty purpose never is o'ertook
     Unless the deed go with it. From this moment
     The very firstlings of my heart shall be
     The firstlings of my hand. And even now,
     To crown my thoughts with acts, be it thought and done:
165  The castle of Macduff I will surprise,
     Seize upon Fife; give to the edge o' th' sword
     His wife, his babes, and all unfortunate souls
     That trace him in his line. No boasting like a fool;
     This deed I'll do before this purpose cool.
170  But no more sights!—Where are these gentlemen?
     Come, bring me where they are.

          *Exeunt.*

A hasty plan is never achieved                                160
unless it is done immediately. From now on,
every deed that my mind imagines
will be carried out by my hand at once. And right now,
to make sure my goals are achieved, let the following deed be
    both thought and done:
I will take Macduff's castle by surprise                      165
and seize Fife; I'll put to the sword
his wife, his children, and all unfortunate souls
who might follow him. No more foolish boasting:
I'll do this deed before my resolve cools off.
But no more visions!—Where are these gentlemen who just
    arrived?
                                                              170
Come on, take me to them.

    *They exit.*

# ACT IV, SCENE II

*Fife. [Macduff's castle.] Enter* MACDUFF'S *wife* [LADY MACDUFF], *her* SON, *and* ROSS.

**LADY MACDUFF**
What had he done, to make him fly the land?

**ROSS**
You must have patience, madam.

**LADY MACDUFF**
                         He had none:
His flight was madness. When our actions do not,
5      Our fears do make us traitors.

**ROSS**
                       You know not
Whether it was his wisdom or his fear.

**LADY MACDUFF**
Wisdom! To leave his wife, to leave his babes,
His mansion and his titles in a place
10    From whence himself does fly? He loves us not;
He wants the natural touch: for the poor wren,
The most **diminutive** of birds, will fight,
Her young ones in her nest, against the owl.
All is the fear and nothing is the love;
15    As little is the wisdom, where the flight
So runs against all reason.

**ROSS**
                   My dearest coz,
I pray you, school yourself. But for your husband,
He is noble, wise, **judicious**, and best knows
20    The fits o' th' season. I dare not speak much further;
But cruel are the times, when we are traitors
And do not know ourselves; when we hold rumour
From what we fear yet know not what we fear,
But float upon a wild and violent sea
25    Each way and move. I take my leave of you.
Shall not be long but I'll be here again.

# ACT 4, SCENE 2

*Fife. A room in Macduff's castle.* LADY MACDUFF, *her* SON, *and* ROSS *enter.*

**LADY MACDUFF**

What has my husband done, to make him flee the land?

**ROSS**

You must be patient, madam.

**LADY MACDUFF**

He was not.
It was madness for him to flee. Even when we've done nothing traitorous,
our fears can make us behave like traitors.                                    5

**ROSS**

You do not know
whether he fled because of his wisdom or his fear.

**LADY MACDUFF**

Wisdom? To abandon his wife, his children,
his mansion, and his possessions, leaving them here
to flee somewhere else? He does not love us.                              10
He lacks natural feeling; for a poor wren,
the smallest of birds, will fight against an owl
to protect the young ones in her nest.
Macduff's actions show nothing but fear, no love for us.
He shows no wisdom, either, since his flight                              15
defies all reason.

**ROSS**

My dearest cousin,
I beg you to control yourself. As for your husband,
he is noble, wise, and sensible, and understands best
the violent disorders of our days. I don't dare speak much further.   20
But these are cruel times when we are regarded as traitors
and do not know the reason for it; when we believe rumors
out of fear, and yet do not understand our fears;
we float upon a wild and violent sea,
at the mercy of its every wave and motion. I'll leave you now.       25
It won't be long before I come again.

Things at the worst will cease, or else climb upward
To what they were before.—My pretty cousin,
Blessing upon you!

**LADY MACDUFF**

30   Fathered he is, and yet he's fatherless.

**ROSS**

I am so much a fool, should I stay longer,
It would be my disgrace and your discomfort:
I take my leave at once.

*Exit* ROSS.

**LADY MACDUFF**

Sirrah, your father's dead;
35   And what will you do now? How will you live?

**SON**

As birds do, Mother.

**LADY MACDUFF**

What, with worms and flies?

**SON**

With what I get, I mean; and so do they.

**LADY MACDUFF**

Poor bird! Thou'dst never fear the net nor lime,*
40   The pitfall nor the gin.

**SON**

Why should I, Mother? Poor birds they are not set for.
My father is not dead, for all your saying.

**LADY MACDUFF**

Yes, he is dead. How wilt thou do for a father?

**SON**

Nay, how will you do for a husband?

**LADY MACDUFF**

45   Why, I can buy me twenty at any market.

**SON**

Then you'll buy 'em to sell again.

---

39   *lime*  birdlime, a sticky substance smeared on tree branches to catch small birds

Things this terrible can't get any worse, or else they'll improve
to what they were before. (*turning to* MACDUFF'S SON) My
    handsome cousin,
God bless you.

**LADY MACDUFF**

He has a father, and yet he's fatherless.                                30

**ROSS**

I am such a fool, if I stay any longer
I'll disgrace myself by weeping, and cause you discomfort.
I'll go at once.

      ROSS *exits.*

**LADY MACDUFF**

Little one, your father's dead.
And what will you do now? How will you live?                   35

**SON**

As birds do, Mother.

**LADY MACDUFF**

What, on worms and flies?

**SON**

On what I can get, I mean—just as they do.

**LADY MACDUFF**

Poor bird, you'll never learn to fear the net, the lime,
the covered pit, or the snare.                                            40

**SON**

Why should I, Mother? They are not set for ordinary birds.
My father is not dead, no matter what you say.

**LADY MACDUFF**

Yes, he is dead. So what will you do for a father?

**SON**

No, what will you do for a husband?

**LADY MACDUFF**

Why, I can buy myself twenty at any market.                    45

**SON**

Then you'll only buy them to sell them again.

**LADY MACDUFF**
Thou speak'st with all thy wit, and yet, i' faith,
With wit enough for thee.

**SON**
Was my father a traitor, Mother?

**LADY MACDUFF**
50  Ay, that he was.

**SON**
What is a traitor?

**LADY MACDUFF**
Why, one that swears and lies.

**SON**
And be all traitors that do so?

**LADY MACDUFF**
Every one that does so is a traitor, and must be hanged.

**SON**
55  And must they all be hanged that swear and lie?

**LADY MACDUFF**
Every one.

**SON**
Who must hang them?

**LADY MACDUFF**
Why, the honest men.

**SON**
Then the liars and swearers are fools; for there are liars and
60  swearers enow to beat the honest men and hang up them.

**LADY MACDUFF**
Now, God help thee, poor monkey!
But how wilt thou do for a father?

**SON**
If he were dead, you'd weep for him. If you would
not, it were a good sign that I should quickly have a
65  new father.

**LADY MACDUFF**

You're speaking with all your wit—and yet I suppose
it's witty enough for a child.

**SON**

Was my father a traitor, Mother?

**LADY MACDUFF**

Yes, he was. 50

**SON**

What is a traitor?

**LADY MACDUFF**

Why, one who swears an oath and breaks it.

**SON**

And are all men who do so traitors?

**LADY MACDUFF**

Every one who does so is a traitor and must be hanged.

**SON**

And must they all be hanged who swear oaths and break them? 55

**LADY MACDUFF**

Every one.

**SON**

Who must hang them?

**LADY MACDUFF**

Why, the honest men.

**SON**

Then the oath-breakers are fools, for there are enough oath-
breakers to beat up the honest men and hang them. 60

**LADY MACDUFF**

Oh, God help you, poor monkey!
But what will you do for a father?

**SON**

If he were dead, you'd weep for him. And if you did not, it would
be a good sign that I'd soon have a new father. 65

**LADY MACDUFF**
    Poor prattler, how thou talk'st!

      *Enter a* MESSENGER.

**MESSENGER**
    Bless you, fair dame! I am not to you known,
    Though in your state of honour I am perfect.
    I doubt some danger does approach you nearly.
70    If you will take a homely man's advice,
    Be not found here. Hence, with your little ones!
    To fright you thus, methinks I am too savage;
    To do worse to you were fell cruelty,
    Which is too nigh your person. Heaven preserve you!
75    I dare abide no longer.

      *Exit* MESSENGER.

**LADY MACDUFF**
                    Whither should I fly?
    I have done no harm. But I remember now
    I am in this earthly world, where to do harm
    Is often **laudable**, to do good sometime
80    Accounted dangerous folly. Why then, alas,
    Do I put up that womanly defence,
    To say I have done no harm?

      *Enter* MURDERERS.

                  What are these faces?

**FIRST MURDERER**
    Where is your husband?

**LADY MACDUFF**
    I hope, in no place so unsanctified
85    Where such as thou mayst find him.

**FIRST MURDERER**
                  He's a traitor.

**SON**
    Thou liest, thou shag-haired villain!

**FIRST MURDERER**
                  What, you egg!

**LADY MACDUFF**

Poor babbler, how you talk!

MESSENGER *enters*.

**MESSENGER**

Bless you, fair lady. You do not know me,
but I am well acquainted with your noble rank.
I fear that some danger is coming very near you.
If you will take an ordinary man's advice,                    70
don't let yourself be found here. Hurry away with your little ones.
I think I'm being heartless to frighten you like this;
but to do worse harm to you would be deadly cruelty,
and yet such harm is very close to you. May heaven save you!
I don't dare stay any longer.                                 75

MESSENGER *exits*.

**LADY MACDUFF**

Where should I flee?
I have done no harm. But now I remember
that I am in this earthly world, where to do harm
is often considered praiseworthy, and to do good is sometimes
considered dangerous foolishness. So why—oh, sorrow!—        80
do I use that womanish defense
of saying I have done no harm?

MURDERERS *enter*.

Whose are these faces?

**FIRST MURDERER**

Where is your husband?

**LADY MACDUFF**

I hope he's in no place so unholy
that the likes of you can find him.                           85

**FIRST MURDERER**

He's a traitor.

**SON**

You lie, you shaggy-haired villain!

**FIRST MURDERER**

What, you brat?

[*Stabbing him.*]

Young fry of treachery!

**SON**

                                 He has killed me, Mother:

90   Run away, I pray you!

      [*Dies.*]

      *Exit* [LADY MACDUFF], *crying "Murder!"* [*followed by*
MURDERERS].

*The* MURDERER *stabs him.*

You fish-spawn of a traitor!

**SON**

He has killed me, Mother:                                    90
Run away, I beg you!

*The* SON *dies.*

LADY MACDUFF *exits, crying "Murder!"* MURDERERS *exit, following her.*

# ACT IV, SCENE III

[*England. Before the King's palace.*] *Enter* MALCOLM
*and* MACDUFF.

**MALCOLM**

Let us seek out some **desolate** shade, and there
Weep our sad bosoms empty.

**MACDUFF**

Let us rather
Hold fast the mortal sword, and like good men
Bestride our down-fall'n birthdom. Each new morn
New widows howl, new orphans cry, new sorrows
Strike heaven on the face, that it resounds
As if it felt with Scotland and yelled out
Like syllable of dolor.

**MALCOLM**

What I believe, I'll wail;
What know, believe; and what I can **redress**,
As I shall find the time to friend, I will.
What you have spoke, it may be so perchance.
This tyrant, whose sole name blisters our tongues,
Was once thought honest; you have loved him well.
He hath not touch'd you yet. I am young; but something
You may deserve of him through me, and wisdom
To offer up a weak, poor, innocent lamb
T' **appease** an angry god.

**MACDUFF**

I am not treacherous.

**MALCOLM**

But Macbeth is.
A good and virtuous nature may recoil
In an imperial charge. But I shall crave your pardon;
That which you are, my thoughts cannot transpose:
Angels are bright still, though the brightest fell.
Though all things foul would wear the brows of grace,
Yet grace must still look so.

# ACT 4, SCENE 3

*England. Before the King's palace.* MALCOLM *and* MACDUFF
*enter.*

**MALCOLM**
Let's find some lonely shade
and weep our sad hearts empty there.

**MACDUFF**
Instead, let us
firmly take hold of a deadly sword, and like good men,     5
fight for our fallen land. Every new morning,
new widows howl, new orphans cry, and new sorrows
strike heaven in the face until it echoes
as if it felt sympathy for Scotland, yelling out
a similar sound of grief.

**MALCOLM**
What I believe, I'll weep for;     10
what I know, I'll believe; and what I can set right,
I will set right, whenever time permits.
What you have said might be true—perhaps.
This tyrant, Macbeth, whose name alone blisters our tongues,
was once thought honorable; you've loved him well yourself.     15
He hasn't harmed you yet. Although I'm only young, you might
earn something from him by doing me harm; and you might think
     it wise
to offer up a weak, poor, innocent lamb like me
to pacify an angry god.

**MACDUFF**
I am not a backstabber.     20

**MALCOLM**
But Macbeth is.
A good and virtuous character may falter
when commanded by a king. But I must ask your pardon.
My thoughts can't change whatever you really are:
angels are still bright, even though the brightest angel fell.     25
If all evil things were to disguise themselves as good,
good things would look the same as always.

**MACDUFF**

I have lost my hopes.

**MALCOLM**

Perchance even there where I did find my doubts.
30 Why in that rawness left you wife and child,
Those precious motives, those strong knots of love,
Without leave-taking? I pray you,
Let not my jealousies be your dishonours,
But mine own safeties. You may be rightly just,
35 Whatever I shall think.

**MACDUFF**

Bleed, bleed, poor country!
Great tyranny, lay thou thy basis sure,
For goodness dare not check thee. Wear thou thy wrongs;
The title is affeered.—Fare thee well, lord.
40 I would not be the villain that thou think'st
For the whole space that's in the tyrant's grasp,
And the rich East to boot.

**MALCOLM**

Be not offended;
I speak not as in absolute fear of you.
45 I think our country sinks beneath the yoke;
It weeps, it bleeds, and each new day a gash
Is added to her wounds. I think withal
There would be hands uplifted in my right;
And here from gracious England have I offer
50 Of goodly thousands. But, for all this,
When I shall tread upon the tyrant's head,
Or wear it on my sword, yet my poor country
Shall have more vices than it had before,
More suffer and more sundry ways than ever,
55 By him that shall succeed.

**MACDUFF**

What should he be?

**MALCOLM**

It is myself I mean, in whom I know
All the particulars of vice so grafted

**MACDUFF**

I have lost hope of gaining your trust.

**MALCOLM**

Perhaps you lost your hopes where I found my doubts.
Why, in such haste, did you leave your wife and child—       30
those precious reasons for staying, those strong knots of love—
without saying farewell? I beg you
not to feel insulted by my suspicions;
they're only for my own safety. You might be perfectly honorable,
no matter what I think.       35

**MACDUFF**

Bleed, bleed, poor country!
Go on and lay a sure foundation, great tyrant,
for good men do not dare to stop you. Flaunt your crimes;
your title is legally upheld.—Farewell, lord.
I wouldn't be the villain that you think I am       40
for all the territories under this tyrant's control—
and the wealthy Orient, as well.

**MALCOLM**

Don't be offended:
I don't say all this because I'm certain that I should fear you.
I think our country sinks beneath its yoke.       45
It weeps, it bleeds, and each new day a gash
is added to its wounds. I also think
that people would lend their hands to defend my right to the
     throne;
and here, the kindly English king has offered to help me
with thousands of men. But despite all this,       50
when I tread upon the tyrant's head
or carry it on my sword, my poor country
will have to endure more vices than it did before;
it will suffer in many ways—and more than ever—
at the hands of Macbeth's successor.       55

**MACDUFF**

Who might he be?

**MALCOLM**

I'm speaking of myself, for I know
that many different vices are grafted onto me;

That, when they shall be opened, black Macbeth
60    Will seem as pure as snow, and the poor state
Esteem him as a lamb, being compared
With my confineless harms.

**MACDUFF**
                                        Not in the legions
Of horrid hell can come a devil more damned
65    In evils to top Macbeth.

**MALCOLM**
                                I grant him bloody,
Luxurious, **avaricious**, false, deceitful,
Sudden, malicious, smacking of every sin
That has a name. But there's no bottom, none,
70    In my **voluptuousness**. Your wives, your daughters,
Your matrons and your maids, could not fill up
The cistern of my lust, and my desire
All continent **impediments** would o'erbear
That did oppose my will. Better Macbeth
75    Than such an one to reign.

**MACDUFF**
                                Boundless intemperance
In nature is a tyranny; it hath been
Th' untimely emptying of the happy throne,
And fall of many kings. But fear not yet
80    To take upon you what is yours. You may
Convey your pleasures in a spacious plenty,
And yet seem cold, the time you may so hoodwink.
We have willing dames enough. There cannot be
That vulture in you, to devour so many
85    As will to greatness dedicate themselves,
Finding it so inclined.

**MALCOLM**
                                With this there grows
In my most ill-composed affection such
A stanchless avarice that, were I King,
90    I should cut off the nobles for their lands,
Desire his jewels and this other's house;
And my more-having would be as a sauce

whenever they bloom, evil Macbeth
will seem as pure as snow, and the poor nation                    60
will regard him as a lamb when his deeds are compared
with my endless crimes.

**MACDUFF**
From all the armies
of horrible hell, there couldn't come a devil damnably
evil enough to surpass Macbeth.                                   65

**MALCOLM**
I agree that he's murderous,
lustful, greedy, treacherous, dishonest,
violent, vicious—having a trace of every sin
that has a name. But there's no bottom—none—
to my lust. Your wives, daughters,                               70
mothers, and virgins could not fill up
the reservoir of my lust—and my desire
would break through all the restraining barriers
that tried to check my will. You'd be better off with Macbeth
than to have someone like me reign.                              75

**MACDUFF**
Unlimited lust
takes terrible control of human nature. It has
suddenly emptied happy thrones,
causing many kings to fall. But still, don't be afraid
to accept what belongs to you. You can                           80
secretly indulge in your pleasures as much as you like,
and still seem chaste; you may blindfold everyone.
We have enough willing ladies. You cannot be
such a vulture that you can devour all the women
willing to give their bodies to a great man                      85
if he should want them.

**MALCOLM**
Along with this, there grows
in my wicked character such
unquenchable greed that, if I were king,
I would take the nobles' lands away,                             90
desiring one man's jewels and another's house;
and the more I took away,

To make me hunger more, that I should forge
Quarrels unjust against the good and loyal,
95    Destroying them for wealth.

**MACDUFF**

This avarice
Sticks deeper, grows with more pernicious root
Than summer-seeming lust, and it hath been
The sword of our slain kings. Yet do not fear.
100    Scotland hath foisons to fill up your will
Of your mere own. All these are portable,
With other graces weigh'd.

**MALCOLM**

But I have none. The king-becoming graces,
As justice, verity, temp'rance, stableness,
105    Bounty, perseverance, mercy, lowliness,
Devotion, patience, courage, fortitude,
I have no relish of them, but abound
In the division of each several crime,
Acting it many ways. Nay, had I pow'r, I should
110    Pour the sweet milk of concord into hell,
Uproar the universal peace, confound
All unity on earth.

**MACDUFF**

O Scotland, Scotland!

**MALCOLM**

If such a one be fit to govern, speak:
115    I am as I have spoken.

**MACDUFF**

Fit to govern?
No, not to live. —O nation miserable!
With an untitled tyrant bloody-sceptered,
When shalt thou see thy wholesome days again,
120    Since that the truest issue of thy throne
By his own **interdiction** stands accursed,
And does blaspheme his breed? Thy royal father
Was a most sainted king. The queen that bore thee,
Oft'ner upon her knees than on her feet,
125    Died every day she lived. Fare thee well!

the greater my appetite would grow, until I provoked
unjust quarrels against good and loyal subjects,
destroying them to get their wealth.                                    95

**MACDUFF**
This greed
is a deeper problem; it grows a more harmful root
than fleeting, youthful lust, and it has put
our kings to the sword. But don't be afraid.
Scotland has enough abundance to satisfy your desires          100
with possessions of your own. All these faults are bearable,
weighed against your virtues.

**MALCOLM**
But I have none. I haven't a trace of kingly virtues
such as justice, truthfulness, self-control, stability,
generosity, perseverance, mercy, humility,                         105
devotion, patience, courage, and resolve;
instead, I excel
in all the different varieties of every crime,
and the many ways to act them out. In fact, if I had power, I would
pour the sweet milk of friendship into hell,                       110
throw the general peace into chaos, and confuse
all order on earth.

**MACDUFF**
Oh, Scotland, Scotland!

**MALCOLM**
If such a man is fit to govern, say so.
I am just what I have told you.                                          115

**MACDUFF**
Fit to govern?
No, not to live.—Oh, what a miserable nation!
With an illegal tyrant wielding a bloody scepter;
when will you see healthy days again,
now that the rightful heir to your throne                          120
stands accursed by his own condemnation,
and insults his ancestors?—Your royal father
was a most saintly king. The queen who bore you
was on her knees praying more often than on her feet,
and prepared herself for heaven every day that she lived. Farewell! 125

These evils thou repeat'st upon thyself
Have banish'd me from Scotland. O my breast,
Thy hope ends here!

**MALCOLM**
                                    Macduff, this noble passion,
130    Child of integrity, hath from my soul
Wiped the black scruples, **reconciled** my thoughts
To thy good truth and honour. Devilish Macbeth
By many of these trains hath sought to win me
Into his power, and modest wisdom plucks me
135    From over-**credulous** haste. But God above
Deal between thee and me! For even now
I put myself to thy direction, and
Unspeak mine own **detraction**, here **abjure**
The taints and blames I laid upon myself,
140    For strangers to my nature. I am yet
Unknown to woman, never was forsworn,
Scarcely have coveted what was mine own,
At no time broke my faith, would not betray
The devil to his fellow, and delight
145    No less in truth than life. My first false speaking
Was this upon myself. What I am truly,
Is thine and my poor country's to command.
Whither indeed, before thy here-approach,
Old Siward, with ten thousand warlike men,
150    Already at a point was setting forth.
Now we'll together, and the chance of goodness
Be like our warranted quarrel! Why are you silent?

**MACDUFF**
Such welcome and unwelcome things at once
'Tis hard to reconcile.

                    *Enter a* DOCTOR.

**MALCOLM**
155    Well, more anon.—Comes the King forth, I pray you?


**DOCTOR**
Ay, sir. There are a crew of wretched souls

These evils of which you have accused yourself
have banished me from Scotland.—Oh, my heart,
your hope ends here!

**MALCOLM**
Macduff, this noble outburst—
born of your integrity—has wiped all black suspicion          130
from my soul, and has fully convinced me
of your truthfulness and honor. Devilish Macbeth
has tried out many plots to win me
into his power, and my prudence prevents me
from trusting anyone hastily. But let God above          135
take charge of our partnership, for I now
put myself under your direction
and take back my own self-accusations, rejecting
the stains and faults I laid upon myself
as foreign to my nature. I am still          140
a virgin, have never perjured myself,
have hardly even wanted my own possessions,
never broke a promise, would not betray
the devil to his fellows, and rejoice
in truth as much as I do in life. My first false words          145
were those I just said about myself. What I truly am
is yours and my poor country's to command;
and indeed, just before you came here,
Old Siward and ten thousand soldiers,
already fully prepared, were setting forth to Scotland.          150
Now we'll go together—and may our chance of success
be as certain as the justice of our cause. Why are you silent?

**MACDUFF**
So many welcome and unwelcome things at once—
it's hard to understand.

> *A* DOCTOR *enters.*

**MALCOLM**
Well, we'll speak more soon. (*to the* DOCTOR) I ask you, is
the King coming this way?          155

**DOCTOR**
Yes, sir. There is a group of wretched souls

That stay his cure. Their malady* convinces
The great assay of art; but at his touch—
Such sanctity hath heaven given his hand—
160    They presently amend.

**MALCOLM**

                              I thank you, doctor.

          *Exit* [DOCTOR].

**MACDUFF**

What's the disease he means?

**MALCOLM**

                                        'Tis call'd the evil:
A most miraculous work in this good king,
165    Which often, since my here-remain in England
I have seen him do. How he solicits heaven,
Himself best knows, but strangely-visited people,
All swoll'n and ulcerous, pitiful to the eye,
The mere despair of surgery, he cures,
170    Hanging a golden stamp about their necks,
Put on with holy prayers; and 'tis spoken,
To the succeeding royalty he leaves
The healing benediction. With this strange virtue,
He hath a heavenly gift of prophecy,
175    And sundry blessings hang about his throne,
That speak him full of grace.

          *Enter* ROSS.

**MACDUFF**

                                        See, who comes here.

**MALCOLM**

My countryman, but yet I know him not.

**MACDUFF**

My ever gentle cousin, welcome hither.

**MALCOLM**

180    I know him now.—Good God, betimes remove
The means that makes us strangers!

---

157    *their malady*  "the King's Evil," scrofula, frequently characterized by an enlarged
       degeneration of lymphatic glands in the neck. The disease was thought to be
       curable at the touch of any king descended from Edward, the Confessor.

waiting for his cure. Their illness defies
the best efforts of medicine, but at his touch—
because heaven has made his hand so holy—
they quickly heal.                                                    160

**MALCOLM**
Thank you, doctor.

       DOCTOR *exits.*

**MACDUFF**
What disease does he mean?

**MALCOLM**
It's called the evil.
This king is able to cure it in a most miraculous way—
and often during my stay here in England,                             165
I have seen him do it. How he appeals to heaven,
he best knows himself; but fearfully diseased people,
who are swollen, covered with sores, pitiful to see,
and beyond the help of medicine, he cures
by hanging a golden coin around their necks                           170
while saying holy prayers. And it's said
that he will leave this healing power
to the kings who come after him. Along with this strange ability,
he has a heavenly gift of prophecy;
and several other blessings surround his throne,                      175
showing him to be full of holiness.

       ROSS *enters.*

**MACDUFF**
Look at who comes here.

**MALCOLM**
It's one of my countrymen, and yet I don't know him.

**MACDUFF**
My most noble cousin, you are welcome here.

**MALCOLM**
I know him now.—Good God, quickly take away                           180
the obstacles that keep us apart!

**ROSS**

Sir, amen.

**MACDUFF**

Stands Scotland where it did?

**ROSS**

Alas, poor country!
185     Almost afraid to know itself. It cannot
Be call'd our mother but our grave, where nothing
But who knows nothing is once seen to smile;
Where sighs and groans, and shrieks that rent the air
Are made, not marked; where violent sorrow seems
190     A modern ecstasy. The dead man's knell
Is there scarce ask'd for who, and good men's lives
Expire before the flowers in their caps,
Dying or ere they sicken.

**MACDUFF**

O, relation too nice, and yet too true!

**MALCOLM**

195     What's the newest grief?

**ROSS**

That of an hour's age doth hiss the speaker;
Each minute teems a new one.

**MACDUFF**

How does my wife?

**ROSS**

Why, well.

**MACDUFF**

200     And all my children?

**ROSS**

Well too.

**MACDUFF**

The tyrant has not battered at their peace?

**ROSS**

No, they were well at peace when I did leave 'em.

**ROSS**

Amen to that, sir.

**MACDUFF**

Has nothing changed in Scotland?

**ROSS**

Oh, sorrow—our poor country
is almost afraid to know itself! It cannot                              185
be called our mother, but our grave; where only those
who know nothing of what's going on are ever seen smiling;
where sighs, groans, and shrieks rip through the air
without being noticed; where violent sorrow seems
an ordinary emotion. One scarcely bothers to ask                       190
what dead man the bell tolls for; and good men
lose their lives before the flowers in their caps lose theirs,
dying before they get sick.

**MACDUFF**

Oh, your description is too precise—and yet too true!

**MALCOLM**

What's the newest grief?                                               195

**ROSS**

A speaker is hissed for describing a grief that happened just an
    hour ago.
Each minute brings a new one.

**MACDUFF**

How is my wife?

**ROSS**

Why, well.

**MACDUFF**

And all my children?                                                   200

**ROSS**

Well too.

**MACDUFF**

The tyrant has not disturbed their peace?

**ROSS**

No, they were well at peace when I left them.

**MACDUFF**
But not a niggard of your speech. How goes 't?

**ROSS**
205  When I came hither to transport the tidings,
Which I have heavily borne, there ran a rumor
Of many worthy fellows that were out;
Which was to my belief witnessed the rather,
For that I saw the tyrant's power afoot.
210  Now is the time of help. Your eye in Scotland
Would create soldiers, make our women fight,
To doff their dire distresses.

**MALCOLM**
                                        Be 't their comfort
We are coming thither. Gracious England hath
215  Lent us good Siward and ten thousand men;
An older and a better soldier none
That Christendom gives out.

**ROSS**
                                        Would I could answer
This comfort with the like! But I have words
220  That would be howled out in the desert air,
Where hearing should not latch them.

**MACDUFF**
                                                    What concern they?
The general cause or is it a fee-grief
Due to some single breast?

**ROSS**
225                              No mind that's honest
But in it shares some woe, though the main part
Pertains to you alone.

**MACDUFF**
                            If it be mine,
Keep it not from me, quickly let me have it.

**ROSS**
230  Let not your ears despise my tongue forever,
Which shall possess them with the heaviest sound
That ever yet they heard.

**MACDUFF**

Don't be stingy with your speech. What's going on?

**ROSS**

When I came here carrying the news                               205
which I have sadly brought, I heard a rumor
that many worthy fellows had taken up arms;
and I believe I witnessed some confirmation of this,
for I saw the tyrant's army on the march.
Now is the time to bring help. Your presence in Scotland
would add more soldiers, and make even our women fight     210
to throw off their fearful troubles.

**MALCOLM**

Let them be comforted,
for we are going there. The King of England has
lent us good Siward and ten thousand men;                       215
no one in the Christian world
is considered an older or better soldier.

**ROSS**

I wish I could respond to
this comfort with more of the same. But I have words to say
that should be howled out in the desert air,                       220
where they might never be heard.

**MACDUFF**

Whom do they concern?
All of Scotland? Or is it a private sorrow
that belongs to some single heart?

**ROSS**

There's not an honest person                                          225
who doesn't share some of the woe—but most of it
concerns you alone.

**MACDUFF**

If it has to do with me,
don't keep it from me. Quickly, tell me about it.

**ROSS**

Don't let your ears despise my tongue forever,              230
for it will make the saddest sound
they've ever yet heard.

**MACDUFF**

                        Humh! I guess at it.

**ROSS**

    Your castle is surprised; your wife and babes

235    Savagely slaughtered. To relate the manner,
    Were, on the quarry of these murdered deer,
    To add the death of you.

**MALCOLM**

                    Merciful heaven!
    —What, man! Ne'er pull your hat upon your brows;

240    Give sorrow words. The grief that does not speak
    Whispers the o'er-fraught heart and bids it break.

**MACDUFF**

    My children too?

**ROSS**

    Wife, children, servants, all that could be found.

**MACDUFF**

    And I must be from thence! My wife killed too?

**ROSS**

245    I have said.

**MALCOLM**

    Be comforted.
    Let's make us med'cines of our great revenge,
    To cure this deadly grief.

**MACDUFF**

    He has no children. All my pretty ones?

250    Did you say "all"? O hell-kite! All?
    What, all my pretty chickens and their dam
    At one fell swoop?

**MALCOLM**

    Dispute it like a man.

**MACDUFF**

                    I shall do so,

255    But I must also feel it as a man.
    I cannot but remember such things were,

**MACDUFF**
Hum! I can guess at it.

**ROSS**
Your castle has been taken by surprise, your wife and children
savagely slaughtered. To give you the details                              235
would mean adding your own death
to this heap of murdered deer.

**MALCOLM**
Merciful heaven!
(*to* MACDUFF) What, man, don't pull your hat down over your
   forehead.
Give words to your sorrow. When grief does not speak aloud,      240
it whispers to the overburdened heart and tells it to break.

**MACDUFF**
My children, too?

**ROSS**
Wife, children, servants—all that could be found.

**MACDUFF**
And I had to be away! My wife was killed too?

**ROSS**
That's what I said.                                                                 245

**MALCOLM**
Be comforted.
Our revenge can be the medicine
to cure this deadly grief.

**MACDUFF**
Macbeth has no children. All my pretty ones?
Did you say "all"? Oh, hellish bird of prey! All?                  250
What, all my pretty babes and their mother,
at one deadly swoop?

**MALCOLM**
Avenge it like a man.

**MACDUFF**
I shall do so,
but I must also feel it like a man.                                        255
I cannot help but remember things

That were most precious to me. Did heaven look on,
And would not take their part? Sinful Macduff,
They were all struck for thee! Naught that I am,
260 Not for their own demerits, but for mine,
Fell slaughter on their souls. Heaven rest them now!

**MALCOLM**
Be this the whetstone of your sword. Let grief
Convert to anger; blunt not the heart, enrage it.

**MACDUFF**
O, I could play the woman with mine eyes
265 And braggart with my tongue! But, gentle heavens,
Cut short all intermission; front to front
Bring thou this fiend of Scotland and myself;
Within my sword's length set him. If he 'scape,
Heaven forgive him too!

**MALCOLM**
270                        This tune goes manly.
Come, go we to the King. Our power is ready;
Our lack is nothing but our leave. Macbeth
Is ripe for shaking, and the powers above
Put on their instruments. Receive what cheer you may.
275 The night is long that never finds the day.

*Exeunt.*

that were most precious to me. Did heaven watch all this
and do nothing to stop it? Sinful Macduff,
they were all killed because of you! Worthless as I am—
it wasn't for their own sins but for mine                                    260
that murder took their souls. Heaven, give them rest now.

**MALCOLM**

Let this be a whetstone to sharpen your sword. Let grief
turn itself into anger. Don't calm your heart; enrage it.

**MACDUFF**

Oh, I could behave like a woman with my weeping eyes,
or a braggart with my tongue! But, gentle heavens,                          265
cut short any delay! Bring this fiend of Scotland
and myself face to face.
Put him within the length of my sword. If he escapes,
may heaven forgive him, too.

**MALCOLM**

This is spoken like a man.                                                   270
Come, let's go to the King. Our army is ready;
we lack nothing except permission to leave. Macbeth
is ripe to be shaken, and even the heavenly powers
are arming themselves. Take whatever comfort you can:
No night is so long that it doesn't end in day.                             275

   *They exit.*

# Act IV Review

## Discussion Questions

1. In Scene i, why is the Witches' chant given in such detail?

2. In your opinion, is Macbeth wise to put his faith in what he learns from the Witches?

3. Why does Macbeth decide to kill Macduff's family? Explain what this shows about Macbeth.

4. How does Malcolm test Macduff?

5. Why do you think Shakespeare included the discussion about the King of England and his special talents in Act IV, Scene iii?

6. Explain your opinion about whether Shakespeare's use of ghosts and apparitions is effective in this play.

7. Why do you think Shakespeare chose to write no more scenes between Macbeth and Lady Macbeth during these last two acts? Explain whether you think this was a good decision or a bad decision.

## Literary Elements

1. Review the ingredients that the Witches put into their cauldron. What might this repulsive stew **symbolize**?

2. What **mood** is created in Act IV, Scene i? Describe some of the things that contribute to this mood.

3. **Hyperbole** means obvious exaggeration. Look at Malcolm's self-description in Act IV, Scene iii, and see if you can find any examples of hyperbole. What is he trying to impress upon Macduff?

4. Remember that **foreshadowing** means the use of hints or clues about what will happen later in the plot. Find at least three examples of foreshadowing in Act IV.

# Writing Prompts

1. On page 194, Malcolm lists the qualities of a good king. Create a chart with the qualities listed down the left side of your paper. Analyze which character would make the best king by checking off the qualities each candidate has demonstrated. For Macbeth, consider his character *before* the murder of Duncan. Compare your results with those of your classmates.

| Qualities of a good king | Macbeth | Duncan | Malcolm | Macduff |
|---|---|---|---|---|
| *justice* | | | ✓ | ✓ |
| | | | | |
| | | | | |
| | | | | |
| | | | | |

2. Imagine that after Lady Macduff discovers that her husband has fled to England, she writes to him expressing her concerns and fears. Write that letter, using the language of Shakespeare.

3. Macduff is torn between his loyalties to his family, country, and king. To what people, beliefs, groups, or organizations do you feel strongly loyal? Write your response in a short essay. Include specific details, examples, and anecdotes that will help others understand your perspective. If you have trouble deciding your priorities, explain why you think that is.

4. Devise a recipe for a "hell-broth" of your own and use the rhythm of the witches' incantation to describe its ingredients ("Scale of dragon, tooth of wolf"). Or, you might feel more angelic and want to come up with a recipe for a brew that is divinely inspired.

# Macbeth

## ACT V

Orson Welles film, 1948

"I will not be afraid of death
and bane till Birnam Forest
come to Dunsinane."

# Before You Read

1. Pay attention to what is troubling Lady Macbeth at the beginning of Act V.

2. Is there any other female character in fiction that Lady Macbeth reminds you of? If so, consider how and why.

3. As you read the last Act, think carefully about who or what is responsible for Macbeth's death.

# Literary Elements

1. **Personification** is a figure of speech in which human characteristics are given to nonhuman things. When Macduff discovers Duncan's dead body, he exclaims "Confusion now hath made his masterpiece" (Act II, Scene iii). Human beings have the ability to kill and create havoc, such as the bloody scene in the royal castle, but abstractions such as "confusion" do not.

2. **Dramatic irony** occurs when the audience knows something that the characters onstage do not. In Act I King Duncan calls Macbeth his "peerless kinsman" and bestows other praise on him, unaware that Macbeth will soon murder him.

3. As you learned in Act I, a **soliloquy** is a long speech that allows characters to reveal their innermost thoughts and feelings to the audience.

# Words to Know

The following vocabulary words appear in Act V in the original text of Shakespeare's play. However, they are words that are still commonly used. Read the definitions here and pay attention to the words as you read the play (they will be in boldfaced type).

| | |
|---|---|
| **abhorred** | despised; loathed |
| **antidote** | cure; remedy |
| **brandished** | shook; flourished |
| **equivocation** | lie; evasion |
| **fortifies** | strengthens; reinforces |
| **industrious** | busy; hard-working |
| **oblivious** | careless; heedless |
| **perilous** | unsafe; hazardous |
| **perturbation** | disturbance; agitation |
| **pristine** | pure; natural |
| **prowess** | bravery; courage |
| **recoil** | flinch; retreat |
| **speculative** | theoretical; unproven |
| **upbraid** | scold; reprimand |

# Act Summary

Back in Scotland, Lady Macbeth has been sinking into madness.

One night, a doctor and a servant stay awake to watch her sleepwalking, trying to rub a spot of imaginary blood off her hand, and raving about her crimes.

Malcolm's English army marches into Scotland, where it unites with Scottish rebels. The friendless Macbeth can no longer trust anyone, and many of his followers are joining the rebels.

Before marching toward Macbeth's castle, Malcolm orders his soldiers to cut down boughs from Birnam Wood to camouflage themselves.

Francesca Annis, Polanski film, 1971

As the army approaches, Macbeth receives word of Lady Macbeth's suicide. Then a messenger brings impossible news—Birnam Wood appears to be approaching Dunsinane! Macbeth senses his impending defeat.

In the field, he meets the vengeful Macduff. Macbeth warns Macduff that he cannot be killed by a man born of a woman. Macduff retorts that he was not born at all, but ripped from his mother's womb.

Macbeth realizes now that he is doomed, but fights on ferociously until Macduff kills him.

Macduff carries Macbeth's severed head to Malcolm, whom he declares King of Scotland. Macbeth's violent reign has ended, and Scotland looks forward to a time of peace and order.

# ACT V, SCENE I

*[Dunsinane. In the castle.] Enter a* DOCTOR *of Physic and a Waiting-*GENTLEWOMAN.

**DOCTOR**

I have two nights watched with you, but can perceive
no truth in your report. When was it she last walked?

**GENTLEWOMAN**

Since his Majesty went into the field, I have seen her rise
from her bed, throw her nightgown upon her, unlock her
5   closet, take forth paper, fold it, write upon 't, read it,
afterwards seal it, and again return to bed; yet all this
while in a most fast sleep.

**DOCTOR**

A great **perturbation** in nature, to receive at once the
benefit of sleep and do the effects of watching! In this
10   slumb'ry agitation, besides her walking and other actual
performances, what, at any time, have you heard her say?

**GENTLEWOMAN**

That, sir, which I will not report after her.

**DOCTOR**

You may to me, and 'tis most meet you should.

**GENTLEWOMAN**

Neither to you nor any one, having no witness to
15   confirm my speech.

*Enter* LADY MACBETH, *with a taper.*

Lo you, here she comes! This is her very guise, and, upon
my life, fast asleep! Observe her; stand close.

**DOCTOR**

How came she by that light?

**GENTLEWOMAN**

Why, it stood by her. She has light by her continually. 'Tis
20   her command.

# ACT 5, SCENE 1

*Dunsinane. Outer room of the castle.* A DOCTOR *and a servant* GENTLEWOMAN *enter.*

**DOCTOR**

For two nights I have watched with you, but I can't see any truth in what you've told me. When was the last time she walked in her sleep?

**GENTLEWOMAN**

Since his Majesty went to the battlefield, I have seen her rise from her bed, throw her dressing gown around her, unlock her chest, take a piece of paper out of it, fold it, write on it, read it,    5 then seal it, and finally go back to bed—and yet remain fast asleep the whole time.

**DOCTOR**

This is a great disorder in her personality—to receive the benefits of sleep, but at the same time to do the deeds of someone awake! In this restless sleep of hers—aside from    10 walking and other actual deeds—what have you heard her say at any time?

**GENTLEWOMAN**

Things, sir, which I must not repeat.

**DOCTOR**

You may repeat them to me—and it's most proper that you should.

**GENTLEWOMAN**

I won't repeat them to you nor anyone else, unless I have a witness to confirm what I say.    15

LADY MACBETH *enters, holding a candle.*

Look—here she comes. This is how she always does it—and by my life, she's fast asleep. Watch her, stand nearby.

**DOCTOR**

How did she get that candle?

**GENTLEWOMAN**

Why, it stood by her bed. She has a candle near her all the time; it's her command.    20

**DOCTOR**
You see, her eyes are open.

**GENTLEWOMAN**
Ay, but their sense is shut.

**DOCTOR**
What is it she does now? Look, how she rubs her hands.

**GENTLEWOMAN**
It is an accustomed action with her, to seem thus washing
25 her hands. I have known her continue in this a quarter of
an hour.

**LADY MACBETH**
Yet here's a spot.

**DOCTOR**
Hark! She speaks. I will set down what comes from her,
to satisfy my remembrance the more strongly.

**LADY MACBETH**
30 Out, damned spot! Out, I say! One. Two. Why, then 'tis
time to do 't. Hell is murky. Fie, my lord, fie! A soldier,
and afeard? What need we fear who knows it, when none
can call our pow'r to account? Yet who would have
thought the old man to have had so much blood in him?

**DOCTOR**
35 Do you mark that?

**LADY MACBETH**
The Thane of Fife had a wife. Where is she now? What,
will these hands ne'er be clean? No more o' that, my lord,
no more o' that! You mar all with this starting.

**DOCTOR**
Go to, go to! You have known what you should not.

**GENTLEWOMAN**
40 She has spoke what she should not, I am sure of that.
Heaven knows what she has known.

**DOCTOR**

You can see that her eyes are open.

**GENTLEWOMAN**

Yes, but her sense of sight is shut.

**DOCTOR**

What is she doing now? Look at how she rubs her hands.

**GENTLEWOMAN**

It's common for her to seem to be washing her hands like
this. I have known her continue this way for a quarter of          25
an hour.

**LADY MACBETH**

There's still a stain here.

**DOCTOR**

Listen. She's speaking. I will write down what she says to help me
remember it better.

**LADY MACBETH**

Out, damned stain! Out, I tell you! One o'clock, two o'clock.        30
Well, then, it's time to do it. Hell is dark. (*as if speaking to*
MACBETH) Shame, my lord, shame—you call yourself a soldier,
and yet you're afraid? Why should we who know about it
be afraid, when we'll be too powerful to be brought to justice?
Still, who would have thought the old man would have so
much blood in him?

**DOCTOR**

Did you hear that?                                                   35

**LADY MACBETH**

Macduff, the Thane of Fife, had a wife. Where is she now? What,
won't these hands ever be clean? (*to* MACBETH) No more of
that, my lord, no more of that. You'll spoil everything with
these outbursts.

**DOCTOR**

For shame, for shame! You have heard a thing you shouldn't
have heard.

**GENTLEWOMAN**

She has said something she shouldn't have said, I am sure of that.   40
Heaven knows what she has done.

**LADY MACBETH**
Here's the smell of the blood still. All the perfumes of
Arabia will not sweeten this little hand. O, O, O!

**DOCTOR**
What a sigh is there! The heart is sorely charged.

**GENTLEWOMAN**
45   I would not have such a heart in my bosom for the dignity
of the whole body.

**DOCTOR**
Well, well, well—

**GENTLEWOMAN**
Pray God it be, sir.

**DOCTOR**
This disease is beyond my practise. Yet I have known those
50   which have walked in their sleep who have died holily in
their beds.

**LADY MACBETH**
Wash your hands. Put on your nightgown. Look not so
pale! I tell you yet again, Banquo's buried. He cannot
come out on 's grave.

**DOCTOR**
55   Even so?

**LADY MACBETH**
To bed, to bed! There's knocking at the gate. Come, come,
come, come, give me your hand! What's done cannot be
undone. To bed, to bed, to bed!

*Exit* LADY [MACBETH].

**DOCTOR**
Will she go now to bed?

**GENTLEWOMAN**
60   Directly.

**DOCTOR**
Foul whisp'rings are abroad. Unnatural deeds
Do breed unnatural troubles. Infected minds
To their deaf pillows will discharge their secrets.

**LADY MACBETH**

The smell of blood is still here. All the perfumes in Arabia will
not sweeten this little hand. Oh, oh, oh!

**DOCTOR**

What a sigh that is! Her heart is heavily burdened.

**GENTLEWOMAN**

I wouldn't have such a heart in my bosom—not for the 45
well-being of all the rest of my body.

**DOCTOR**

Well, well, well.

**GENTLEWOMAN**

I pray to God it turns out well, sir.

**DOCTOR**

This disease is too much for my skills. Still, I have known people
who have walked in their sleep, and then died religiously 50
in their beds.

**LADY MACBETH** *(to* MACBETH*)*

Wash your hands. Put on your dressing gown. Don't look so pale.
I tell you yet again, Banquo is buried; he cannot come out of
his grave.

**DOCTOR**

Am I really hearing this? 55

**LADY MACBETH**

To bed, to bed. There's knocking at the gate. Come, come, come,
come. Give me your hand. What's been done cannot be undone
To bed, to bed, to bed.

LADY MACBETH *exits.*

**DOCTOR**

Will she go to bed now?

**GENTLEWOMAN**

Immediately. 60

**DOCTOR**

Ugly rumors are spreading. Unnatural crimes
bring on unnatural rebellions. Diseased minds
will confess their secrets to their deaf pillows.

More needs she the divine than the physician.
65 God, God forgive us all! Look after her;
Remove from her the means of all annoyance,
And still keep eyes upon her. So, good night.
My mind she has mated and amazed my sight.
I think, but dare not speak.

**GENTLEWOMAN**
70 Good night, good doctor.

*Exeunt.*

She is in more need of a priest than a physician.
God, God, forgive us all. Watch over her.                              65
Take away anything she might use to harm herself,
and always keep your eyes on her. And so, good night.
She has bewildered my mind and amazed my sight.
I don't dare say what I'm thinking.

**GENTLEWOMAN**

Good night, good doctor.                                               70

    *They exit.*

# ACT V, SCENE II

*[The country near Dunsinane.] Drum and colours. Enter*
MENTEITH, CAITHNESS, ANGUS, LENNOX, *and*
SOLDIERS.

**MENTEITH**

The English power is near, led on by Malcolm,
His uncle Siward and the good Macduff.
Revenges burn in them; for their dear causes
Would to the bleeding and the grim alarm
5     Excite the mortified man.

**ANGUS**

                   Near Birnam Wood
Shall we well meet them; that way are they coming.

**CAITHNESS**

Who knows if Donalbain be with his brother?

**LENNOX**

For certain, sir, he is not. I have a file
10     Of all the gentry. There is Siward's son,
And many unrough youths that even now
Protest their first of manhood.

**MENTEITH**

                  What does the tyrant?

**CAITHNESS**

Great Dunsinane he strongly **fortifies**:
15     Some say he's mad; others, that lesser hate him
Do call it valiant fury, but, for certain,
He cannot buckle his distempered cause
Within the belt of rule.

**ANGUS**

                Now does he feel
20     His secret murders sticking on his hands;
Now minutely revolts **upbraid** his faith-breach.
Those he commands move only in command,
Nothing in love. Now does he feel his title
Hang loose about him, like a giant's robe
25     Upon a dwarfish thief.

# ACT 5, SCENE 2

*The country near Dunsinane. Drum and colors.* MENTEITH,
CAITHNESS, ANGUS, LENNOX, *and* SOLDIERS *enter.*

**MENTEITH**
The English army is near—led by Malcolm,
his uncle Siward, and the good Macduff.
They burn with desire for revenge, for their heartfelt reasons
would stir even a dead man to join the bloody, grim attack.     5

**ANGUS**
We'll meet them as we should
near Birnam Wood. They're coming that way.

**CAITHNESS**
Does anyone know if Donalbain is with his brother Malcolm?

**LENNOX**
I am certain that he is not, sir. I have a list
of all the nobles. Siward's son is there,     10
and many beardless youths that want
to prove themselves men for the first time.

**MENTEITH**
What's the tyrant Macbeth doing?

**CAITHNESS**
He's fortifying great Dunsinane Castle.
Some say that he's mad; others, who hate him less,     15
say that he's full of valiant fury. But it's certain
that he can't buckle his diseased and bloated cause
within the belt of his control.

**ANGUS**
Now he feels
the blood of his secret murders sticking to his hands.     20
Every minute, new revolts protest his treason.
The men he commands follow him only because he commands
    them,
not because they love him. Now he feels his kingship
hanging loosely on him, like a giant's robe
on a dwarfish thief.     25

**MENTEITH**
    Who then shall blame
His pestered senses to **recoil** and start,
When all that is within him does condemn
Itself for being there?

**CAITHNESS**
30                        Well, march we on,
To give obedience where 'tis truly owed.
Meet we the med'cine of the sickly weal,
And with him pour we in our country's purge
Each drop of us.

**LENNOX**
35                  Or so much as it needs,
To dew the sovereign flower and drown the weeds.
Make we our march towards Birnam.

    *Exeunt, marching.*

**MENTEITH**
Who can blame
his tormented nerves for recoiling and trembling
when, with his whole mind, he condemns himself
for being alive?

**CAITHNESS**
Well, let's march on                                    30
and give obedience to whom we really owe it.
We'll meet Malcolm, the healer of our sick country;
and with his help, we'll pour out every last drop of our blood
to purge our country of evil.

**LENNOX**
Or as much blood as is needed                           35
to nourish the royal flower of healing, and to drown the weeds.
Let us march towards Birnam Wood.

    *They exit, marching.*

# ACT V, SCENE III

[*Dunsinane. A room in the castle.*] *Enter* MACBETH, DOCTOR, *and* ATTENDANTS.

**MACBETH**

Bring me no more reports. Let them fly all!
Till Birnam Wood remove to Dunsinane
I cannot taint with fear. What's the boy Malcolm?
Was he not born of woman? The spirits that know
5   All mortal consequences have pronounced me thus:
"Fear not, Macbeth; no man that's born of woman
Shall e'er have power upon thee." Then fly, false thanes,
And mingle with the English epicures.
The mind I sway by and the heart I bear
10   Shall never sag with doubt nor shake with fear.

*Enter a* SERVANT.

The devil damn thee black, thou cream-faced loon!
Where got'st thou that goose look?

**SERVANT**

There is ten thousand—

**MACBETH**

Geese, villain?

**SERVANT**

15                                                 Soldiers, sir.

**MACBETH**

Go prick thy face and over-red thy fear,
Thou lily-liver'd boy. What soldiers, patch?
Death of thy soul! Those linen cheeks of thine
Are counselors to fear. What soldiers, whey-face?

**SERVANT**

20   The English force, so please you.

**MACBETH**

Take thy face hence.

*Exit* SERVANT.

Seyton!—I am sick at heart,

# ACT 5, SCENE 3

*Dunsinane. A room in the castle.* MACBETH, DOCTOR, *and* SERVANTS *enter.*

**MACBETH**
Don't bring me any more reports. Let all my thanes desert me!
Until Birnam Wood approaches Dunsinane,
I'll not weaken with fear. Who is this boy Malcolm?
Wasn't he born to a woman? The spirits who know
the future of all human events have told me this:       5
"Never fear, Macbeth. No man that's born to a woman
will ever have power over you." So flee, treacherous thanes,
and join with the soft, well-fed Englishmen.
The mind that rules me and the heart I bear
will never give way to doubt or shake with fear.       10

*A* SERVANT *enters.*

May the devil blacken you with damnation, you cream-faced idiot!
Why do you look as white as a goose?

**SERVANT**
There are ten thousand—

**MACBETH**
Geese, you villain?

**SERVANT**
Soldiers, sir.       15

**MACBETH**
Go stick pins in your face and hide your fear in blood,
you cowardly boy. What soldiers, clown?
Death upon your soul! Those linen-white cheeks of yours
will make others afraid. What soldiers, milk-face?

**SERVANT**
The English army, may it please you.       20

**MACBETH**
Take your face away.

SERVANT *exits.*

Seyton!—I am sick at heart

When I behold—Seyton, I say!—This push
Will cheer me ever, or disseat me now.
I have lived long enough. My way of life
Is fall'n into the sear, the yellow leaf,
And that which should accompany old age,
As honour, love, obedience, troops of friends,
I must not look to have; but, in their stead,
Curses, not loud but deep, mouth-honour, breath,
Which the poor heart would fain deny, and dare not.
　　　Seyton!

*Enter* SEYTON.

**SEYTON**
What's your gracious pleasure?

**MACBETH**
　　　　　　　　　　　What news more?

**SEYTON**
All is confirmed, my lord, which was reported.

**MACBETH**
I'll fight, till from my bones my flesh be hacked.
Give me my armour.

**SEYTON**
　　　　　　'Tis not needed yet.

**MACBETH**
I'll put it on.
Send out more horses; skirr the country round;
Hang those that talk of fear. Give me mine armour.
How does your patient, doctor?

**DOCTOR**
　　　　　　　　　　　Not so sick, my lord,
As she is troubled with thick-coming fancies,
That keep her from her rest.

**MACBETH**
　　　　　　　　Cure her of that.
Canst thou not minister to a mind diseased,
Pluck from the memory a rooted sorrow,

when I look—Seyton, I say!—This effort
will encourage me forever or dethrone me now.
I have lived long enough. My way of life                          25
has grown withered, its leaves have turned yellow,
and things which should come with old age,
such as honor, love, obedience, and many friends,
I cannot hope to have; instead, I must expect
curses that are not loud but deep, lip-service, and hollow        30
    declarations of loyalty
which my poor heart cannot believe, but must.—
Seyton!

       SEYTON *enters.*

**SEYTON**
What is your Highness's pleasure?

**MACBETH**
What more news is there?

**SEYTON**
All reports have been confirmed, my lord.                        35

**MACBETH**
I'll fight until my flesh has been hacked from my bones.
Give me my armor.

**SEYTON**
It's not needed yet.

**MACBETH**
I'll put it on.
Send out more horsemen. Scour the countryside.                   40
Hang anyone who says he's afraid. Give me my armor.—
How is your patient doing, doctor?

**DOCTOR**
My lord, she's not so much sick
as troubled with frequent hallucinations,
which keep her from getting any rest.                             45

**MACBETH**
Cure her of that.
Can't you treat a diseased mind,
pull up a rooted sorrow from the memory,

Raze out the written troubles of the brain

50 And with some sweet **oblivious antidote**
Cleanse the stuff'd bosom of that **perilous** stuff
Which weighs upon the heart?

**DOCTOR**

Therein the patient
Must minister to himself.

**MACBETH**

55 Throw physic to the dogs, I'll none of it.—
Come, put mine armour on. Give me my staff.
Seyton, send out.—Doctor, the thanes fly from me.—
Come, sir, dispatch.—If thou couldst, doctor, cast
The water of my land, find her disease,

60 And purge it to a sound and **pristine** health,
I would applaud thee to the very echo,
That should applaud again.—Pull 't off, I say.—
What rhubarb, senna, or what purgative drug,
Would scour these English hence? Hear'st thou of them?

**DOCTOR**

65 Ay, my good lord. Your royal preparation
Makes us hear something.

**MACBETH**

Bring it after me.
I will not be afraid of death and bane,
Till Birnam Forest come to Dunsinane.

*[Exeunt* MACBETH *and* SEYTON.*]*

**DOCTOR** *[aside]*

70 Were I from Dunsinane away and clear,
Profit again should hardly draw me here.

*Exit.*

erase the troubles engraved on the brain,
and with some sweet, forgetfulness-inducing medicine,                    50
clean the over-packed bosom of that dangerous stuff
which weighs against the heart?

**DOCTOR**

In such things,
the patient must treat himself.

**MACBETH**

Then throw medical science to the dogs. I'll have none of it.          55
(*to* SEYTON) Come, put my armor on me. Give me my staff.

> SERVANTS *begin to arm him.*

Seyton, send commands.—Doctor, the thanes are fleeing me.—
Go on, Seyton, hurry.—Doctor, if you could test
the urine of my kingdom and find out what disease it has,
then purge it until it's in sound, perfect health,                     60
I'd applaud you until my applause
came back as an echo. (*to* SEYTON) Pull off my armor, I say.
(*to* DOCTOR) What rhubarb, senna, or other purgative drug,
would clean these English out of here? Have you heard about
   them?

**DOCTOR**

Yes, my good lord. Because of your royal preparations for battle,    65
we've all heard something about them.

**MACBETH** (*to* SEYTON)

Bring my armor after me.—
I will not be afraid of death and destruction
until Birnam Forest comes toward Dunsinane.

**DOCTOR** (*aside*)

If I could get far away from Dunsinane,                                 70
I wouldn't come back here again even for good pay.

> *They exit.*

# ACT V, SCENE IV

[*Country near Birnam Wood.*] *Drum and colours. Enter*
MALCOLM, SIWARD, MACDUFF, YOUNG SIWARD,
MENTEITH, CAITHNESS, ANGUS, *and* SOLDIERS,
*marching.*

**MALCOLM**
Cousins, I hope the days are near at hand
That chambers will be safe.

**MENTEITH**
We doubt it nothing.

**SIWARD**
What wood is this before us?

**MENTEITH**
5 The Wood of Birnam.

**MALCOLM**
Let every soldier hew him down a bough
And bear 't before him. Thereby shall we shadow
The numbers of our host and make discovery
Err in report of us.

**SOLDIERS**
10 It shall be done.

**SIWARD**
We learn no other but the confident tyrant
Keeps still in Dunsinane and will endure
Our setting down before 't.

**MALCOLM**
'Tis his main hope;
15 For where there is advantage to be gone,
Both more and less have given him the revolt,
And none serve with him but constrained things
Whose hearts are absent too.

**MACDUFF**
Let our just censures
20 Attend the true event, and put we on
**Industrious** soldiership.

# ACT 5, SCENE 4

*Country near Birnam Wood. Drum and banners.* MALCOLM,
SIWARD, MACDUFF, YOUNG SIWARD, MENTEITH, CAITHNESS,
ANGUS, *and* SOLDIERS *enter, marching.]*

**MALCOLM**
Kinsmen, I hope the days are coming soon
when we'll be safe in our own home.

**MENTEITH**
We don't doubt it.

**SIWARD**
What woods are these in front of us?

**MENTEITH**
It's Birnam Wood.                                                     5

**MALCOLM**
Let every soldier cut down a bough
and carry it in front of him. That way, we will hide
the size of our army, and Macbeth's lookouts
will give incorrect reports of us.

**SOLDIERS**
It will be done.                                                       10

**SIWARD**
All we have learned is that the confidant tyrant
is keeping himself inside Dunsinane castle, and will stay there
when we arrive before it.

**MALCOLM**
That's his best hope;
for whenever they've had the opportunity,                              15
men of both lesser and greater ranks have revolted against him,
and those who continue to serve him do so only by force,
for their hearts aren't with him, either.

**MACDUFF**
Let's not make guesses about the situation
until the battle is over; meanwhile, let's get to work               20
like true soldiers.

**SIWARD**
                         The time approaches
That will with due decision make us know
What we shall say we have and what we owe.
25    Thoughts **speculative** their unsure hopes relate,
But certain issue strokes must arbitrate;
Towards which advance the war.

        *Exeunt, marching.*

**SIWARD**
The time is coming
when we'll learn the difference
between what we say we have and what we really have.
Mere guesswork tells us about nothing except our uncertain     25
    hopes;
the final outcome must be decided by the strokes of swords;
so let our army advance toward that outcome.

    *They exit, marching.*

# ACT V, SCENE V

[*Dunsinane. Within the castle.*] *Enter* MACBETH,
SEYTON, *and* SOLDIERS, *with drum and colours.*

**MACBETH**

Hang out our banners on the outward walls.
The cry is still "They come!" Our castle's strength
Will laugh a siege to scorn. Here let them lie
Till famine and the ague eat them up.
5      Were they not forced with those that should be ours,
We might have met them dareful, beard to beard,
And beat them backward home.

*A cry within of women.*

What is that noise?

**SEYTON**

It is the cry of women, my good lord.

[*Exit.*]

**MACBETH**

10    I have almost forgot the taste of fears.
The time has been, my senses would have cooled
To hear a night-shriek, and my fell of hair
Would at a dismal treatise rouse and stir
As life were in 't. I have supped full with horrors;
15    Direness, familiar to my slaughterous thoughts
Cannot once start me.

[*Enter* SEYTON.]

Wherefore was that cry?

**SEYTON**

The Queen, my lord, is dead.

**MACBETH**

She should have died hereafter;
20    There would have been a time for such a word.*
Tomorrow, and tomorrow, and tomorrow
Creeps in this petty pace from day to day,

---

19-20  *She . . . word* She would have died sometime.

236    *Macbeth*

# ACT 5, SCENE 5

*Dunsinane. Inside the castle.* MACBETH, SEYTON, *and* SOLDIERS *enter with drums and banners.*

**MACBETH**

Hang our banners on the outside walls.
Word keeps coming that they're on their way. Our castle's strength
will make a mockery of their siege. Let them wait outside
until they're finished off by starvation and illness.
If they weren't reinforced by deserters from our side,    5
we might have met them boldly in the battlefield, face to face,
and beat them until they fled back home.

*Women are heard crying offstage.*

What is that noise?

**SEYTON**

It is women crying, my good lord.

    SEYTON *exits.*

**MACBETH**

I have almost forgotten what it feels like to be afraid.    10
There was a time when I would have shivered
to hear a shriek at night; and if I'd heard a frightening tale,
the hair on my scalp would have risen and stirred
as if it were alive. I have eaten my fill of horrors.
Terror is so familiar to my murderous thoughts    15
that it can't startle me anymore.

    SEYTON *reenters.*

What was that crying about?

**SEYTON**

The Queen is dead, my lord.

**MACBETH**

She should have died at another time.
There would have been a better moment for such news.    20
Tomorrow, and the day after, and the day after—
the days creep on one after another at a dismal pace

To the last syllable of recorded time;
And all our yesterdays have lighted fools
25 The way to dusty death. Out, out, brief candle!
Life's but a walking shadow, a poor player
That struts and frets his hour upon the stage
And then is heard no more. It is a tale
Told by an idiot, full of sound and fury,
30 Signifying nothing.

*Enter a* MESSENGER.

Thou com'st to use thy tongue; thy story quickly!

**MESSENGER**
Gracious my lord,
I should report that which I say I saw,
But know not how to do it.

**MACBETH**
35                                       Well, say, sir.

**MESSENGER**
As I did stand my watch upon the hill,
I look'd toward Birnam, and anon, methought,
The wood began to move.

**MACBETH**
                              Liar and slave!

**MESSENGER**
40 Let me endure your wrath, if 't be not so.
Within this three mile may you see it coming;
I say, a moving grove.

**MACBETH**
                              If thou speak'st false,
Upon the next tree shalt thou hang alive,
45 Till famine cling thee. If thy speech be sooth,
I care not if thou dost for me as much.
I pull in resolution, and begin
To doubt th' **equivocation** of the fiend
That lies like truth: "Fear not, till Birnam Wood
50 Do come to Dunsinane!" And now a wood
Comes toward Dunsinane. Arm, arm, and out!
If this which he avouches does appear,

until the last word of time's record is spoken;
and all our yesterdays have lighted the way for fools
to die and turn to dust. Out, out, brief candle!                    25
Life is just a walking shadow, a bad actor
who struts and worries for an hour on stage,
and then is heard no more. It is a tale
told by an idiot, full of sound and fury,
but meaning nothing.                                                30

     *A* MESSENGER *enters.*

You came to use your tongue; tell your story quickly.

**MESSENGER**
My gracious lord,
I should report to you what I think I saw,
but I don't know how to do it.

**MACBETH**
Well, tell me, sir.                                                 35

**MESSENGER**
As I stood watch on the hill,
I looked toward Birnam, and it soon appeared to me
as if the woods began to move.

**MACBETH**
Liar and villain!

**MESSENGER**
Let me suffer from your anger if it's not true.                     40
You can see it coming, less than three miles away.
I tell you, it's a moving forest.

**MACBETH**
If you are lying,
you'll hang alive on the nearest tree
until you starve. If you're telling the truth,                      45
I don't care if you do the same to me.—
My courage falters, and I begin
to fear the trickery of the devil,
for he tells lies that seem true. "Don't be afraid till Birnam Wood
comes to Dunsinane!"—and now the woods                              50
are coming toward Dunsinane.—To arms, to arms, let's attack!—
If what this man tells me is really true,

There is nor flying hence nor tarrying here.
I 'gin to be aweary of the sun,
55    And wish th' estate o' th' world were now undone.
Ring the alarum-bell! Blow, wind! Come wrack!
At least we'll die with harness on our back.

    *Exeunt.*

neither running away nor waiting here is possible.
I'm beginning to grow weary of sunlight,
and wish that the universe itself were wiped away.— 55
Sound the call to arms!—Let winds blow, let destruction come;
at least we'll die with armor on our backs.

    *They exit.*

# ACT V, SCENE VI

*[Dunsinane. Before the castle.] Drum and colours. Enter*
MALCOLM, SIWARD, MACDUFF, *and their* ARMY,
*with boughs.*

**MALCOLM**
Now near enough. Your leafy screens throw down.
And show like those you are. You, worthy uncle,
Shall, with my cousin, your right noble son,
Lead our first battle. Worthy Macduff and we
5    Shall take upon 's what else remains to do,
According to our order.

**SIWARD**
                                   Fare you well.
Do we but find the tyrant's power tonight,
Let us be beaten, if we cannot fight.

**MACDUFF**
10   Make all our trumpets speak; give them all breath,
Those clamorous harbingers of blood and death.

*Exeunt. Alarums continued.*

# ACT 5, SCENE 6

*In front of the castle at Dunsinane. Drums and banners.*
*MALCOLM, SIWARD, MACDUFF, and their* ARMY *enter, carrying*
*branches.*

**MALCOLM**
Now we are near enough. Throw down your leafy coverings,
and look like yourselves.—My worthy Uncle Siward,
you and my cousin, your most noble son,
will lead our first battalion. Worthy Macduff and I
shall undertake whatever else remains to be done,                    5
according to our battle plan.

**SIWARD**
Farewell.
If we can find the tyrant's army tonight,
let us be beaten if we don't put up a fight.

**MACDUFF**
Make all our trumpets speak; give breath                             10
to those noisy announcers of blood and death.

*They exit. The battle sounds continue.*

# ACT V, SCENE VII

[*Another part of the field.*] *Enter* MACBETH.

**MACBETH**
They have tied me to a stake; I cannot fly,
But bear-like, I must fight the course.* What's he
That was not born of woman? Such a one
Am I to fear, or none.

*Enter* YOUNG SIWARD.

**YOUNG SIWARD**
5    What is thy name?

**MACBETH**
                                    Thou'lt be afraid to hear it.

**YOUNG SIWARD**
No, though thou call'st thyself a hotter name
Than any is in hell.

**MACBETH**
                                    My name's Macbeth.

**YOUNG SIWARD**
10    The devil himself could not pronounce a title
More hateful to mine ear.

**MACBETH**
                                    No, nor more fearful.

**YOUNG SIWARD**
Thou liest, **abhorred** tyrant; with my sword
I'll prove the lie thou speak'st.

*Fight, and* YOUNG SIWARD *slain.*

**MACBETH**
15                                    Thou wast born of woman
But swords I smile at, weapons laugh to scorn,
**Brandished** by man that's of a woman born.

*Exit.*

*Alarums. Enter* MACDUFF.

---

2    *bear-like . . . course* A popular sport of Shakespeare's time was bearbaiting, in
which a bear was chained to a stake in a ring or arena and ferocious dogs were
released to attack him. *Course* was a common term for *bout.*

# ACT 5, SCENE 7

*Another part of the field.* MACBETH *enters.*

**MACBETH**
They have tied me to a stake. I cannot flee,
but must fight out this round like a bear. Where is a man
who was not born to a woman? I'm supposed to fear
such a man, or no one.

YOUNG SIWARD *enters.*

**YOUNG SIWARD**
What is your name?                                          5

**MACBETH**
You will be afraid to hear it.

**YOUNG SIWARD**
No—not even if you call yourself by a hotter name
than any in hell.

**MACBETH**
My name is Macbeth.

**YOUNG SIWARD**
The devil himself could not speak a name                    10
more hateful to my ear.

**MACBETH**
No, nor one more frightening.

**YOUNG SIWARD**
You lie, detested tyrant. With my sword,
I'll prove that what you say is a lie.

*They fight, and* YOUNG SIWARD *is slain.*

**MACBETH**
You were born to a woman.                                   15
I smile at swords, and laugh scornfully at any weapons
wielded by a man who was born to a woman.

*Exit.*

*Battle sounds.* MACDUFF *enters.*

**MACDUFF**

That way the noise is. Tyrant, show thy face!
If thou be'st slain and with no stroke of mine,
20    My wife and children's ghosts will haunt me still.
I cannot strike at wretched kerns, whose arms
Are hired to bear their staves. Either thou, Macbeth,
Or else my sword with an unbatter'd edge
I sheathe again undeeded. There thou shouldst be;
25    By this great clatter, one of greatest note
Seems bruited. Let me find him, Fortune!
And more I beg not.

     *Exit. Alarums.*

     *Enter* MALCOLM *and* SIWARD.

**SIWARD**

This way, my lord. The castle's gently render'd.
The tyrant's people on both sides do fight;
30    The noble thanes do bravely in the war;
The day almost itself professes yours,
And little is to do.

**MALCOLM**

               We have met with foes
That strike beside us.

**SIWARD**

35                 Enter, sir, the castle.

     *Exeunt. Alarum.*

**MACDUFF**

    The noise of battle is that way. Tyrant, show your face!
    If you are killed, and not by a stroke of my sword,
    my wife and children's ghosts will always haunt me.      20
    I cannot fight against wretched mercenaries, whose arms
    have been hired to carry their spears. I must fight you, Macbeth—
    or else I'll sheathe my unused sword,
    its edge still unbattered. You ought to be there;
    all this noise seems to report the presence      25
    of someone important. Let me find him, Fortune!
    I beg for nothing more.

        *They exit while the trumpets sound the call to arms.*

        MALCOLM *and* SIWARD *enter.*

**SIWARD**

    Come this way, my lord. The castle has surrendered without a
        fight;
    the tyrant's people are fighting for both sides;
    the noble thanes are proving themselves brave in battle;      30
    victory almost declares itself yours,
    and there is little left to do.

**MALCOLM**

    We have met with foes
    who deliberately miss us.

**SIWARD**

    Sir, enter the castle.      35

        *They exit. Battle sounds.*

# ACT V, SCENE VIII

[*Another part of the field.*] *Enter* MACBETH.

**MACBETH**
Why should I play the Roman fool* and die
On mine own sword? Whiles I see lives, the gashes
Do better upon them.

*Enter* MACDUFF.

**MACDUFF**
                                        Turn, hell-hound, turn!

**MACBETH**
5    Of all men else I have avoided thee.
But get thee back! My soul is too much charged
With blood of thine already.

**MACDUFF**
                                        I have no words;
My voice is in my sword, thou bloodier villain
10   Than terms can give thee out!

*Fight. Alarum.*

**MACBETH**
                                        Thou losest labor:
As easy mayst thou the intrenchant air
With thy keen sword impress as make me bleed.
Let fall thy blade on vulnerable crests;
15   I bear a charmed life, which must not yield,
To one of woman born.

**MACDUFF**
                                        Despair thy charm
And let the angel whom thou still hast served
Tell thee, Macduff was from his mother's womb
20   Untimely ripped.*

**MACBETH**
Accursed be that tongue that tells me so,

---

1    *Roman fool* Roman gentlemen traditionally committed suicide to avoid dishonor
in defeat.

20   *Untimely ripped* i.e., Caesarian section, the operation of taking a child from the
uterus by cutting through the walls of the abdomen

# ACT 5, SCENE 8

*Another part of the field.* MACBETH *enters.*

**MACBETH**
Why should I play the Roman fool and die
on mine own sword? While I see living men, wounds
are better on them than on me.

    MACDUFF *enters.*

**MACDUFF**
Turn this way, hellhound, turn this way!

**MACBETH**
I have avoided you more than any other man.     5
But get back from me. My soul is already too burdened
with your family's blood.

**MACDUFF**
I have nothing to say;
my voice is in my sword, you villain—too murderous
to be described in words.     10

    *They fight. Battle sounds.*

**MACBETH**
You're wasting your strength.
You'd find it just as easy to damage the intangible air
with your sword as to make me bleed.
Let your blade fall on vulnerable heads;
I live a charmed life that cannot be lost     15
to a man born to a woman.

**MACDUFF**
Lose hope for your charmed life,
and let the demon you've been serving
tell you that Macduff was prematurely ripped
from his mother's womb.     20

**MACBETH**
May the tongue that tells me so be cursed,

For it hath cowed my better part of man!
And be these juggling fiends no more believed,
That palter with us in a double sense;
25  That keep the word of promise to our ear,
And break it to our hope. I'll not fight with thee.

#### MACDUFF

Then yield thee, coward,
And live to be the show and gaze o' th' time:
We'll have thee, as our rarer monsters are,
30  Painted upon a pole and under writ
"Here may you see the tyrant."

#### MACBETH

                                        I will not yield,
To kiss the ground before young Malcolm's feet,
And to be baited with the rabble's curse.
35  Though Birnam Wood be come to Dunsinane,
And thou opposed, being of no woman born,
Yet I will try the last. Before my body
I throw my warlike shield. Lay on, Macduff;
And damned be him that first cries, 'Hold, enough!'

*Exeunt, fighting. Alarums.*

*They enter fighting, and* MACBETH *is slain.* [*Exit*
MACDUFF, *with* MACBETH.] *Retreat and flourish.*
*Enter, with drum and colours,* MALCOLM, SIWARD,
ROSS, THANES, *and* SOLDIERS.

#### MALCOLM
40  I would the friends we miss were safe arrived.

#### SIWARD

Some must go off; and yet, by these I see,
So great a day as this is cheaply bought.

#### MALCOLM

Macduff is missing, and your noble son.

#### ROSS

Your son, my lord, has paid a soldier's debt.
45  He only lived but till he was a man;

for it has daunted my manly spirit!
And let no one else believe those cheating devils
who trick with us with their double meanings,
standing by the letter of their promises,                                          25
but breaking our hopes with them. I won't fight with you.

**MACDUFF**

Then surrender, coward,
and live on to be the carnival attraction of the age.
Just as we do with the rarest freaks, we'll paint your picture
on a banner and hang it from a pole; and under the picture
    we'll write,                                                 30
"Here you can see the tyrant."

**MACBETH**

I won't surrender
to kiss the ground before young Malcolm's feet,
and be tormented by the curses of the rabble.
Though Birnam Wood has come to Dunsinane,                                           35
and I'm faced with you, a man not born to a woman,
I'll test fate one last time. I hold up my warrior's shield
in front of my body. Fight on, Macduff,
and may the first one to cry, "Stop! Enough!" be damned.

    *They exit, fighting. Battle sounds.*

    *They reenter fighting.* MACBETH *is slain.* MACDUFF *exits,*
    *carrying off* MACBETH'S *body. Trumpets sound the call for a*
    *retreat. Fanfare.* MALCOLM, SIWARD, ROSS, *the other* THANES
    *and* SOLDIERS *enter with drums and banners.*

**MALCOLM**

I wish the friends we're missing had arrived safely.                                40

**SIWARD**

Some of them must have died; and yet, judging from the
    number of survivors I see,
our great victory today has been won with few lives.

**MALCOLM**

Macduff is missing, and your noble son.

**ROSS**

My lord, your son has paid a soldier's debt.
He only lived until he was a man—                                                   45

The which no sooner had his **prowess** confirmed
In the unshrinking station where he fought,
But like a man he died.

**SIWARD**

Then he is dead?

**ROSS**

50    Ay, and brought off the field. Your cause of sorrow
Must not be measured by his worth, for then
It hath no end.

**SIWARD**

Had he his hurts before?

**ROSS**

Ay, on the front.

**SIWARD**

55    Why then, God's soldier be he!
Had I as many sons as I have hairs,
I would not wish them to a fairer death;
And so, his knell is knolled.

**MALCOLM**

He's worth more sorrow,
60    And that I'll spend for him.

**SIWARD**

He's worth no more.
They say he parted well and paid his score,
And so God be with him! Here comes newer comfort.

*Enter* MACDUFF, *with* MACBETH's *head.*

**MACDUFF**

Hail, King! For so thou art: behold, where stands
65    Th' usurper's cursed head. The time is free.
I see thee compassed with thy kingdom's pearl,
That speak my salutation in their minds,
Whose voices I desire aloud with mine:
Hail, King of Scotland!

and as soon as had he proved himself a man with his bravery,
fighting at his post without shrinking,
he died like a man.

**SIWARD**

Then he is dead?

**ROSS**

Yes, and carried off the field. You must not grieve          50
enough to match his value; if you do,
your grief will never end.

**SIWARD**

Were his wounds in front of him?

**ROSS**

Yes, on his front.

**SIWARD**

Well, then—let him be God's soldier now!          55
If I had as many sons as I have hairs,
I couldn't wish finer deaths for them;
that's all the tolling he'll get for his funeral.

**MALCOLM**

He deserves more sorrow,
and I'll give it to him.          60

**SIWARD**

He's worth no more.
They say he departed well and paid up his bill—
and so, God be with him. Here comes further comfort.

MACDUFF *reenters, carrying* MACBETH's *head.*

**MACDUFF**

Hail, King!—for that's what you are. Look—here stands
the tyrant's accursed head. The world is free from evil.          65
I see that you are surrounded by the noblest men of your
    kingdom,
who are thinking the same greeting I now make.
I wish to hear all our voices say it aloud:
Hail, King of Scotland!

**ALL**

70                              Hail, King of Scotland!

    *Flourish.*

**MALCOLM**

We shall not spend a large expense of time
Before we reckon with your several loves,
And make us even with you. My thanes and kinsmen,
Henceforth be earls, the first that ever Scotland
75      In such an honour named. What's more to do,
Which would be planted newly with the time—
As calling home our exiled friends abroad
That fled the snares of watchful tyranny,
Producing forth the cruel ministers
80      Of this dead butcher and his fiend-like queen,
Who, as 'tis thought, by self and violent hands
Took off her life—this, and what needful else
That calls upon us, by the grace of Grace,
We will perform in measure, time, and place.
85      So, thanks to all at once and to each one,
Whom we invite to see us crown'd at Scone.

    *Flourish. Exeunt Omnes.*

    *FINIS.*

**ALL**

    Hail, King of Scotland!                                                 70

      *Fanfare.*

**MALCOLM**

    I shall not waste much time
    before I reward each of you for your services,
    so that I don't remain in your debt. My thanes and kinsmen,
    from now on you will be called earls—the first men ever honored
    by that title in Scotland. There's more to be done,      75
    which should be carried out quickly to begin our new age;
    for example, we'll call home from abroad our exiled friends
    who fled to escape the shrewd tyrant;
    and we'll bring to justice the cruel agents
    of this dead butcher and his fiendish queen—      80
    who, it is believed, took her life
    by her own violent hands. Whatever else
    we are called upon to do, we shall carry it out fully,
    at the proper time and place, by the grace of God.
    So thanks to all of you together, and to each one of you—    85
    and we invite you to see us crowned at Scone.

      *Fanfare. All exit.*

# Act V Review

## Discussion Questions

1. Describe Lady Macbeth's mental state at the beginning of this act. Does this come as a surprise or was this possibility part of her character from the beginning? Explain.

2. In Act V, Macbeth is trapped in his castle in Dunsinane. Discuss some of the ways in which this setting enhances the ideas and actions of the play.

3. How does Macbeth receive the news of his wife's death?

4. What is Macbeth's attitude toward the final battle?

5. How does Macduff reveal Macbeth's doom?

6. Is there any point in this act in which you feel sympathy for Macbeth? Explain your answer.

7. Explain how the Witches' prophecies were filled.

## Literary Elements

1. **Personification** means giving human characteristics to nonhuman things. Look at the Doctor's speech at the end of Act V, Scene i. What examples of personification do you find? Explain what is gained by this figure of speech.

2. **Dramatic irony** occurs when the audience has important knowledge that the main characters lack. Explain the irony on page 232 when the soldiers are ordered to cut down tree branches.

3. Macbeth's **soliloquy** in Scene v is famous. Read lines 19–30 again and discuss any phrases you find that are memorable. What do they reveal about Macbeth's state of mind?

# Writing Prompts

1. Write a dialogue that might occur between Lady Macbeth and a therapist.

2. Macbeth's defeat and Malcolm's ascent to the throne seem to be evidence that Shakespeare believes bad deeds are punished and good deeds rewarded. Do you believe this is true? Explain in writing whether people usually "get what they deserve." Give examples to support your conclusion.

3. Write out the battle plan for Malcolm's assault on Macbeth's castle (Scene vi). Remember, conquering an 11th-century castle was no easy task: these fortresses were built of stone and wood and often positioned on a hill or surrounded by a moat. Think of the plans made by Malcolm's forces, and consider other actions they might have had to resort to. Make sure to include a map.

4. Write a scene in which the Witches hash over the final battle. Remember to include actions with your dialogue.

5. In Scene i, the Gentlewoman explains how she has seen Lady Macbeth write on some paper and then seal it and go back to bed. Whom do you think she has written to, and what has she written about? Write the letter you think Lady Macbeth wrote in her sleep.

# The Play in Review

## Discussion and Analysis

1. Do the Macbeths really care for each other or are they only interested in themselves? Using examples from the text, discuss how the relationship between the Macbeths develops during the play.

2. Why do you think the Witches choose Macbeth for their victim? Would Banquo have served their purpose just as well?

3. Throughout the play, there are references to double meanings and opposites. In Act I, Scene i, the Witches say, "Fair is foul, and foul is fair." In Act I, Scene iii, Macbeth echoes that with "So foul and fair a day I have not seen." Find more examples of double meanings and opposites in the text. Why do you think Shakespeare carefully weaves these references throughout the play?

4. If Macbeth had not killed Duncan, do you think that he would still have become king?

5. Where is Fleance? Explain what you think happened to him.

6. Identify some situations in today's world where the struggle for power has led to violence. Can you name some world leaders, past or present, that resemble Macbeth in their methods to gain control and remain in power?

# Literary Elements

1. Why is it **ironic** that Lady Macbeth goes mad and kills herself? (Remember, irony is the opposite of what might be expected.) Explain your response.

2. What do you think is the overriding message, or **theme**, of the play?

3. A **tragedy** is a serious work of literature that narrates the events leading to the downfall of a **tragic hero**, who is usually of noble birth. His or her downfall is a result of a **tragic flaw** or fatal character weakness. Think about how Macbeth fits this definition. What is his tragic flaw?

4. *Macbeth* is rich in **conflicts**. Elements of the plot, characters, setting, and language add to the play's conflict and move the plot forward. Name one of the conflicts in the play that contributes to the tragedy.

5. Shakespeare is fond of using **personification**, the technique of attributing human traits to something that is not human. For example, in Act IV, Scene iii, Malcolm says, "I think our country sinks beneath the yoke; / It weeps, it bleeds, and each new day a gash / Is added to her wounds." Of course, a country cannot really weep or bleed. Find an example of personification in the text that you find striking and share it with the class, explaining its use if necessary.

6. *Macbeth* is filled with **imagery**—word pictures that appeal to the five senses (sight, hearing, taste, touch, and smell) and add emotion and power to the writing. To see how imagery is embedded into the play, find and list some of the images of blood, light, darkness, and fire you see. What is their dramatic purpose?

# Writing Prompts

1. Write a short parody of *Macbeth*.

2. Who is the stronger character, Macbeth or Lady Macbeth? Write an opinion essay that explains your choice.

3. After viewing any film version of *Macbeth*, write a review. Good choices to see include Orson Welles' *Macbeth*, Roman Polanski's *Macbeth*, or (if you enjoy a challenge) the great Japanese director Akira Kurosawa's film *Throne of Blood*.

4. Do some research on any of the following subjects and write a short report on your findings. You may start with an encyclopedia but at least one of your sources should include a text about either 11th-century Scotland (the time of the play) or 16th-century England (Shakespeare's time).

   a. superstition and witchcraft
   b. Scottish weapons and warfare
   c. history of the Scots or Picts
   d. religion and science in 11th-century Scotland
   e. King James I
   f. Roman attempts to conquer Scotland
   g. Elizabethan theaters
   h. special effects of the Elizabethan stage
   i. King Macbeth

5. Write a letter to the director of a local theatrical company suggesting that *Macbeth* be their next production. Give specific reasons for your choice.

# Multimodal and Group Activities

1.   Divide into two teams, affirmative and negative, and debate one of the following resolutions.

     **Resolved:** Family members influence an individual's actions more than anything else.

     **Resolved:** Free will is a stronger force than fate.

2.   Find a long passage from the play that you find especially powerful. Everyone in a group should take one line to memorize, thinking of all the meaning and emotion contained in each idea of that line. Then, seated or kneeling in a circle, each person can read his or her line in the correct order, giving the passage the maximum amount of drama and feeling it deserves.

3.   Pretend you are the casting director for a new production of *Macbeth*. Choose modern actors for the main characters, thinking carefully about why an actor fits a character in the play. You may then design a playbill or poster advertising your production, using imagery, typography, and language that gives the audience some idea of the way you will interpret this version of "the Scottish play."

4.   Find a work of art based on *Macbeth*, such as a musical piece, a play, or a painting. In an oral presentation to your group or class, explain how the music, drama, or art captures the mood and events of the play. You may need to use a VCR, boom box, or slides to share this work with your audience.

5.   Design costumes for some of the characters in *Macbeth*. Using the resources of the Internet or a library, examine the dress of royalty, nobles, commoners, merchants, warriors, and clergy. How were witches conceived in 11th-century Scotland? Sketch the garments you design or make replicas for puppets or paper dolls. Another way to show your creations would be by using cartoon panels or computer graphics.

# Shakespeare's Life

Many great authors can be imagined as living among the characters in their works. Historical records reveal how these writers spoke, felt, and thought. But Shakespeare is more mysterious. He never gave an interview or wrote an autobiography—not even one of his letters survives. What we know about his life can be told very briefly.

Shakespeare was born in April 1564. The exact date of his birth is unknown, but he was baptized on April 26 in the Stratford-upon-Avon church. His father, John, was a prominent local man who served as town chamberlain and mayor. Young William attended

grammar school in Stratford, where he would have learned Latin—a requirement for a professional career—and some Greek.

In 1582, William married Anne Hathaway. He was 18; she was 26. At the time of their marriage, Anne was already three months pregnant with their first daughter, Susanna. In 1585, the couple had twins, Judith and Hamnet. Hamnet died before reaching adulthood, leaving Shakespeare no male heir.

Even less is known about Shakespeare's life between 1585 and 1592. During that time, he moved to London and became an actor and playwright. He left his family behind in Stratford. Although he surely visited them occasionally, we have little evidence about what Shakespeare was like as a father and a husband.

Several of his early plays were written during this time, including *The Comedy of Errors*, *Titus Andronicus*, and the three parts of *Henry VI*. In those days, working in the theater was rather like acting in soap operas today—the results may be popular, but daytime series aren't recognized as serious art. In fact, many people were opposed to even allowing plays to be performed. Ministers warned their congregations of the dangers of going to plays.

But Shakespeare and his friends were lucky. Queen Elizabeth I loved plays. She protected acting companies from restrictive laws and gave them her permission to perform. Shakespeare wrote several plays to be performed for the queen, including *Twelfth Night*.

Queen Elizabeth I

After Elizabeth's death in 1603, Shakespeare's company became known as the King's Men. This group of actors performed for James I, who had ruled Scotland before becoming the King of England. Perhaps to thank James for his patronage, Shakespeare wrote *Macbeth*, which included two topics of strong interest to the king—Scottish royalty and witchcraft.

Unlike many theater people, Shakespeare actually earned a good living. By 1599, he was part owner of the Globe, one of the newest theaters in London. Such plays as *Othello*, *Hamlet*, and *King Lear* were first performed there.

The Globe

In 1610 or 1611, Shakespeare moved back to the familiar surroundings of Stratford-upon-Avon. He was almost 50 years old, well past middle age by 17th-century standards. Over the years, he'd invested in property around Stratford, acquiring a comfortable estate and a family coat of arms.

But Shakespeare didn't give up writing. In 1611, his new play *The Tempest* was performed at court. In 1613, his play *Henry VIII* premiered. This performance was more dramatic than anyone expected. The stage directions called for a cannon to be fired when "King Henry" came on stage. The explosion set the stage on fire, and the entire theater burned to the ground.

Shakespeare died in 1616 at the age of 52. His gravestone carried this inscription:

> **Good friend for Jesus sake forbear**
> **To dig the dust enclosed here!**
> **Blest be the man that spares these stones,**
> **And curst be he that moves my bones.**

This little verse, so crude that it seems unlikely to be Shakespeare's, has intrigued countless scholars and biographers.

Anyone who loves Shakespeare's plays and poems wants to know more about this author. Was he a young man who loved Anne Whateley but was forced into a loveless marriage with another Anne? Did he teach school in Stratford, poach Sir Thomas Lucy's deer, or work for a lawyer in London? Who is the "dark lady" of his sonnets?

But perhaps we are fortunate in our ignorance. Orson Welles, who directed an all-black stage production of *Macbeth* in 1936, put it this way: "Luckily, we know almost nothing about Shakespeare . . . and that makes it so much easier to understand [his] works . . . It's an egocentric, romantic, 19th-century conception that the artist is more interesting and more important than his art."

In Shakespeare's world, there can be little question of which is truly important, the work or the author. Shakespeare brings up the curtain and then steps back into the wings, trusting the play to a cast of characters so stunningly vivid that they sometimes seem more real than life.

# Shakespeare's Theater

In Shakespeare's London, a day's entertainment often began with a favorite amusement, bearbaiting. A bear would be captured and chained to a stake inside a pit. A pack of dogs would be released, and they would attack the bear. Spectators placed bets on which would die first. Admission to these pits cost only a penny, so they were very popular with working-class Londoners.

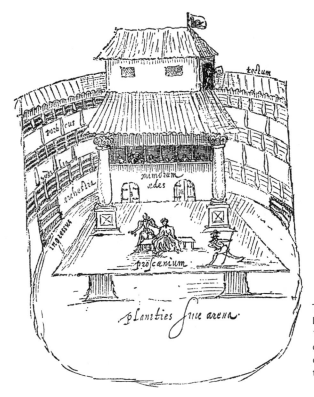

The Swan Theatre in London, drawn in 1596, the only known contemporary image of an Elizabethan theater interior

After the bearbaiting was over, another penny purchased admission to a play. Each theater had its own company of actors, often supported by a nobleman or a member of the royal family. For part of his career, Shakespeare was a member of the Lord

Chamberlain's Men. After the death of Queen Elizabeth I, King James I became the patron of Shakespeare's company. The actors became known as the King's Men.

As part owner of the Globe Theatre, Shakespeare wrote plays, hired actors, and paid the bills. Since the Globe presented a new play every three weeks, Shakespeare and his actors had little time to rehearse or polish their productions. To complicate matters even more, most actors played more than one part in a play.

Boys played all the female roles. Most acting companies had three or four youths who were practically raised in the theater. They started acting as early as age seven and played female roles until they began shaving. Shakespeare had a favorite boy actor (probably named John Rice) who played Cleopatra and Lady

Richard Tarleton, Elizabethan actor famous for his clowning

Macbeth. Actresses would not become part of the English theater for another fifty years.

The audience crowded into the theater at about 2 p.m. The cheapest seats weren't seats at all but standing room in front of the stage. This area, known as the "pit," was occupied by "groundlings" or "penny knaves," who could be more trouble to the actors than they were worth. If the play was boring, the groundlings would throw rotten eggs or vegetables. They talked loudly to their friends, played cards, and even picked fights with one another. One theater was set on fire by audience members who didn't like the play.

The theater was open to the sky, so rain or snow presented a problem. However, the actors were partially protected by a roof known as the "heavens," and wealthier patrons sat in three stories of sheltered galleries that surrounded the pit and most of the main stage.

**Shakespeare's Theater**

The main stage, about 25 feet deep and 45 feet wide, projected into the audience, so spectators were closely involved in the action. This stage was rather bare, with only a few pieces of furniture. But this simplicity allowed for flexible and fluid staging. Unlike too many later productions, plays at the Globe did not grind to a halt for scene changes. When one group of actors exited through one doorway and a new group entered through another, Shakespeare's audience understood that a new location was probably being represented.

Behind the main stage was the "tiring-house," where the actors changed costumes. Above the stage was a gallery that, when it wasn't occupied by musicians or wealthy patrons, could suggest any kind of high place—castle ramparts, a cliff, or a balcony.

Special effects were common. A trapdoor in the main stage allowed ghosts to appear. Even more spectacularly, supernatural beings could be lowered from above the stage. For added realism, actors hid bags of pig's blood and guts under their stage doublets. When pierced with a sword, the bags spilled out over the stage and produced a gory effect.

All these staging methods and design elements greatly appealed to Elizabethan audiences and made plays increasingly popular. By the time Shakespeare died in 1616, there were more than thirty theaters in and around London.

What would Shakespeare, so accustomed to the rough-and-tumble stagecraft of the Globe, think of the theaters where his plays are performed today? He would probably miss some of the vitality of the Globe. For centuries now, his plays have been most often performed on stages with a frame called the "proscenium arch," which cleanly separates the audience from the performers. This barrier tends to cast a peculiar shroud of privacy over his plays so that his characters do not seem to quite enter our world.

But with greater and greater frequency, Shakespeare's plays are being performed out-of-doors or in theaters with three- or four-sided stages. And a replica of the Globe Theatre itself opened in London in 1996, only about 200 yards from the site of the original.

The new Globe Theatre, London

This new Globe is an exciting laboratory where directors and actors can test ideas about Elizabethan staging. Their experiments may change our ideas about how Shakespeare's plays were performed and give new insights into their meaning.

# The Globe Theatre

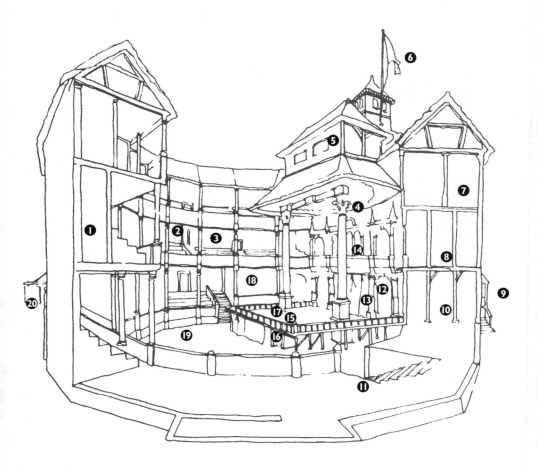

1 **Corridor** A passageway serving the middle gallery.

2 **Entrance** Point leading to the staircase and upper galleries.

3 **Middle Gallery** The seats here were higher priced.

4 **The Heavens** So identified by being painted with the zodiac signs.

5 **Hut** A storage area that also held a winch system for lowering characters to the stage.

6    **Flag**  A white flag above the theater meant a show that day.

7    **Wardrobe**  A storage area for costumes and props.

8    **Dressing Rooms**  Rooms where actors were "attired" and awaited their cues.

9    **Tiring-House Door**  The rear entrance or "stage door" for actors or privileged spectators.

10   **Tiring-House**  Backstage area providing space for storage and costume changes.

11   **Stairs**  Theatergoers reached the galleries by staircases enclosed by stairwells.

12   **Stage Doors**  Doors opening into the Tiring-House.

13   **Inner Stage**  A recessed playing area often curtained off except as needed.

14   **Gallery**  Located above the stage to house musicians or spectators.

15   **Trapdoor**  Leading to the "Hell" area, where a winch elevator was located.

16   **Hell**  The area under the stage, used for ghostly comings and goings or for storage.

17   **Stage**  Major playing area jutting into the Pit, creating a sense of intimacy.

18   **Lords Rooms** or private galleries.  Six pennies let a viewer sit here, or sometimes on stage.

19   **The Pit**  Sometimes referred to as "The Yard," where the "groundlings" watched.

20   **Main Entrance**  Here the doorkeeper collected admission.

## IMAGE CREDITS

The Kobal Collection/Columbia: 13. ©Sunset Boulevard/CORBIS: 16.
The Kobal Collection: 19. John Vickers, London: 108; Kurt E. Schon, Ltd.: 158.
The Kobal Collection/Republic: 210. ©Pawel Libera/CORBIS: 269

Clipart.com : 4 (top), 5, 8, 11, 264, 266, 267. Library of Congress 4 (bottom), 263.
Photofest: 6, 7, 68, 71, 111, 213.